e

e

y

THE POTTER NEEDLEWORK LIBRARY

machine embroidery

Clare Carter

Photography by Linda Burgess

Clarkson Potter/Publishers
New York

pages 1: Button Collection (see page 62)
page 5: Pins with Panache (see page 82)

Illustrations • Kate Simunek

Text, design and layout copyright © 1996 Quadrille Publishing Limited
Project photography copyright © 1996 Linda Burgess
Detail photography copyright © 1996 Dave King

Published by Clarkson N. Potter/Publishers, 201 East 50th Street, New York, NY 10022. Member of the Crown Publishing Group.

Random House, Inc. New York, Toronto, London, Sydney, Auckland
http://www.randomhouse.com

CLARKSON N. POTTER, POTTER, and colophon are trademarks of Clarkson N. Potter, Inc.

Originally published in Great Britain by Quadrille Publishing Limited in 1996.

Manufactured in Spain.

Library of Congress Cataloging-in-Publication data is available upon request.

ISBN 0-517-88719-3

10 9 8 7 6 5 4 3 2 1

First American Edition

contents

Introduction

Using a sewing machine to create decorative stitching effects is a wonderful way of embellishing fabric. The embroidered effect can be as simple as using a contrasting thread for top stitching or as intricate as a fine tapestry with a multitude of precisely placed tiny stitches.

This book is designed to be a general introduction to machine embroidery: the informative first chapter reacquaints the reader with the sewing machine, offers a guide to fabrics, threads, and useful sewing accessories and includes a practical section on transferring designs. The next chapter, which includes the first designs to stitch, uses the machine set up for normal sewing but introduces the idea of stitching for decoration rather than solely to join or finish a fabric edge. The third chapter is about free-motion embroidery, in which the fabric is moved in any direction by hand rather than backward or forward by the machine. The progression of designs in this section starts with those using simple lines of stitching, gradually builds up to solid areas of color, introduces the idea of altering the stitch tension, and culminates in the creation of a joyful figurative picture. The final chapter includes a section on lettering, explains how to use vanishing fabrics, and finishes with further tension effects.

Each project or design in the book is supported by a techniques section that fully explains the machine embroidery methods used. This makes the projects easier to work, while at the same time giving readers the necessary skills to use the methods for their own designs. The final section of the book includes small patterns for practicing free-motion stitching techniques, as well as some alternative designs and alphabets.

This book is written for anyone with access to a sewing machine. The combination of desirable finished objects, each decorated with machine embroidery, with easily accessible technical information and useful problem-solving sections should make machine embroidery as approachable as other, more traditional, forms of needlework.

Getting started

Machine embroidery is both intriguing and frightening. Picking up a needle and thread to embroider by hand seems an easier entry into decorative stitching than using a sewing machine, but both are creative needlecrafts, and the great advantage of machine embroidery is that the machine forms the stitches, allowing the embroiderer to concentrate entirely on the design. Moreover, while bending over a whirring sewing machine is perhaps not quite as peaceful as stitching by hand, working a project in machine embroidery does become a fascinating and utterly absorbing process.

All the projects and techniques in this book can be worked on a simple zigzag-stitch machine – there is no need for an electronic or computerized model, so anyone with access to an electrically operated sewing machine can experiment with machine embroidery. Besides this, machine embroidery requires few other tools or accessories, and any well-stocked workbasket should provide all the necessary basic equipment.

sewing machines

The machine embroidery techniques and projects in this book are designed to be produced on a fairly basic sewing machine. The designs in the Set-stitch Decoration chapter could all, with only one or two minor changes, be stitched with a straight-stitch machine. For the designs in the Free-motion Stitching and Decorative Effects chapters, a swing-needle (zigzag-stitch) machine is helpful, but not essential. Read through the information below to refamiliarize yourself with the sewing machine and its different parts, but do not think of it as a shopping list – the latest computerized machine may be desirable, but such a machine is not necessary to create any of the designs in this book.

Types of machine

An electrically operated sewing machine, which leaves both hands free to control the fabric, is essential for free-motion embroidery. There are many different types on the market, offering a range of facilities within each price bracket.

• All modern machines have a swing-needle bar, which means that they can do zigzag as well as straight stitching.

• Semi-automatic and automatic machines will have a variety of utility stitches as well as zigzag. The stitching patterns may be altered manually by inserting a specific cam, or the cams may be built in and selected by switching a lever or a button.

• Electronic machines will offer a high degree of control over the moving parts within the machine, since the position of the needle relative to the movement of the feed and the speed of stitching are all precisely coordinated.

• Computerized machines offer a huge variety of pre-programmed stitch effects, and often have memory facilities that allow individual adjustments to be stored and repeated.

• The two most important settings to check when considering a machine for free-motion embroidery are those controlling the feed movement and the tension of the stitches.

1 face plate
2 tension dial
3 width control/pattern selector
4 stitch-length dial
5 presser foot thumb screw
6 needle bar
7 thread guide
8 needle (throat) plate
9 feed teeth
10 bed plate
11 shuttle-cover plate
12 reverse-stitch lever

Feed

When a machine is set for normal stitching, the feed automatically moves the fabric under the needle. For free-motion stitching or embroidery, the fabric must be moved by hand, so you will need to be able to disconnect or immobilize the feed movement (see page 44). Most swing-needle machines will offer a darning or embroidery option, and this will include some facility for lowering or covering the feed teeth.

Tension settings

Some machine manuals advise against altering the tension, but it does no harm to the machine, and minor adjustments are often necessary to achieve perfect stitching. For free-motion stitching, more adjustments may be desired. It is possible to alter the tension on a machine with universal tension, but be sure to refer to the manual, and make a record of the original settings so that the machine can be reset correctly.

needle thread   BALANCED TENSION

bobbin thread

fig 1

TOP TENSION TOO TIGHT

fig 2

TOP TENSION TOO LOOSE

fig 3

Setting the tension
To check the tension for either set or free-motion stitching, thread the needle and bobbin with contrasting colors, and stitch a few lines of straight stitching.
• If needle-thread and bobbin tensions are correct, no contrasting thread will appear on either side of the fabric (fig 1).
• If the bobbin thread appears on the top surface of the fabric (fig 2), first loosen the needle-thread tension, stitch, and check again. If the thread still appears, tighten the bobbin tension, and stitch again. Continue to loosen or tighten until a perfect stitch is achieved.
• If the needle thread is being pulled to the underside of the fabric (fig 3), first tighten the needle-thread tension, check by stitching, then loosen the bobbin tension and recheck. Continue adjusting to achieve a perfect tension, and note the tension settings before adjusting to create different effects.

Needle-thread tension It is easier to alter the needle-thread tension, so start by adjusting here. On most machines, the needle-thread tension is set by moving a dial on which the higher numbers represent a tighter tension. Normal tension for set stitching is between 3 and 5. Some machines will simply have + or − signs, with normal in the middle.

Bobbin tension Your machine may have either a vertical bobbin case or a horizontal bobbin case, which is often fixed in the shuttle race.
• On a vertical bobbin case, the tension is adjusted by a small tension screw (fig 4). There may also be a larger screw that holds the case together. If there are no + or − signs, turn the tension screw clockwise to tighten the tension and counterclockwise to loosen it. It is easy to unscrew the screw completely and lose it, so work over a piece of cloth that will catch it if it drops.
• A built-in horizontal bobbin case will usually have a tension screw facing upward underneath the slide plate (fig 5). Many will have a numbered scale or + and − signs; if not, note the angle of the screw head before adjusting.

fig 4

fig 5

Needles

Machine embroidery requires sharp, strong needles. If a needle is having trouble stitching through thick or heavily worked fabric, move up a size.

Needles are sold in a combination of English/US and Continental sizes:

English/US
8   9   10 11 12 14 16 18 20
Continental
60 65 70 75 80 90 100 110 120

There are various types of needle.
Standard needle Should be thicker for embroidery than for seaming.
Ballpoint needle Useful for stitching synthetic fabrics or if the machine is skipping stitches.

Jeans needle Tapered and with a very sharp point. Useful for embroidering on tough fabrics.
Topstitch needle Has a larger eye that will accommodate a heavier thread.
Twin needle Available in a variety of sizes that are marked with a double figure, for example 3/80. The first is millimeters between needles, the second the actual needle size. It makes narrow double lines of stitching that can be used for spaghetti quilting (see page 35).
Wing needle Has a spear-shaped head that leaves a hole on the right fabric. (loose weave)

Machine feet

Free-motion machine embroidery is often stitched without a foot, or with a darning foot if preferred, but the feet listed below are common attachments that are useful for decorative stitching.

Presser foot Basic foot suitable for straight and zigzag stitching.
Open-toe presser foot Comes in a transparent plastic version that offers the maximum view of decorative set stitch embroidery.
Embroidery foot Wide space underneath this foot allows for a build-up of decorative stitches, and the grooves underneath make stitching curves much easier.
Darning foot Usually spring loaded, allowing it to bounce over uneven raised surfaces.

Pintuck foot Useful for working even rows of twin-needle pintucks.
Tailor-tacking foot Stitches loops that can be used for faggoting or fringes.
Zipper foot Can be moved to left or right of needle, allowing stitching to run very close to teeth of a zipper or other raised surface. A central needle position, used for straight stitch only, is useful for machine quilting.
Cording foot Useful for couching work. A whole in the front of the foot insures that the cord is fed into the correct position to be stitched over.

darning foot

zipper foot

cording foot

open-toe presser foot   pintuck foot

Machine maintenance

Specific machine-care tips are given for the various embroidery techniques throughout the book, but a little time spent on general maintenance for your machine will greatly enhance its performance.

• Clean your machine regularly; using it for embroidery means that it will be stitching for longer periods, and machine embroidery threads are softer than sewing threads and create more fluff and lint, so regular brushing and declogging of the shuttle race and all mechanical parts is essential.

• Refer to your sewing-machine manual for oiling instructions. Older machines need to be oiled frequently, but some newer ones are self lubricating and applying oil to them might adversely affect their performance. Use only sewing-machine oil, and after oiling, stitch on scrap cloth for a minute or so to insure that no excess oil is going to seep out onto the fabric.

• When using the machine for free-motion embroidery projects, work in 20-minute spells or less to prevent the machine engine from overheating.

fabrics & threads

There are no set rules for machine embroidery. It does not require special canvas or evenweave fabric, and designs can be worked with ordinary sewing threads or with special embroidery threads. The guidelines below are intended to help new embroiderers, or to suggest alternatives or solutions if the fabric or threads that have been tried do not produce a satisfactory effect.

Fabrics

Fabrics that have an even weave, in which the threads are regularly spaced and cross at right angles, will be the easiest to embroider because they have the same amount of give in both directions and can easily be stretched tightly in an embroidery hoop. But it should be possible to embroider on almost any fabric by following the tips below.

For set-stitch decoration

If machine embroidery is being used to decorate the fabric but not to obscure it, as in set-stitch decoration, the fabric should be chosen purely for its decorative qualities and its suitability for the finished purpose. The embroidered decoration is worked using set-stitching techniques – that is, with the sewing machine set up for normal stitching – so the decorative stitching should pose no extra problems.

For free-motion stitching without a foot

Fabrics that are to be stitched using a free-motion machine-embroidery technique must be stretched tight in an embroidery hoop to provide a firm base for stitching (see pages 16 and 50).

Free-motion stitching techniques vary greatly. If the stitching is to cover little of the fabric surface, the fabric must be chosen for its looks and purpose, and as long as it is a firmly woven fabric that can be stretched tightly in a hoop, it will be possible to embroider it. On the other hand, if the fabric is to be entirely covered with embroidery, it will be the foundation for a great many stitches and must be strong. An evenly woven cloth made from natural fiber, such as calico, is ideal for this.

Natural fibers tend to be stronger than synthetics and will separate to allow the needle through. Silk is an ideal fabric for free-motion stitching, since it comes in a wealth of colors, weights, and finishes, can be stretched tightly in a hoop, and is stronger than cotton.

With a synthetic fabric, the needle is more likely to cut a hole through the fibers. These, and shiny fabrics, are more difficult to stitch than others, but the stitching problems can usually be overcome by using new, sharp needles or a ballpoint needle.

Very fine or sheer fabrics, such as organza, can be used in a double layer – laid over or even bonded to a stronger, neutral-colored base fabric. Lightweight fabrics can be backed with a stabilizer (see opposite). KNIT

Try basting stretch fabrics to calico with numerous rows of cross-basting, before stretching in a hoop. Stitching on stretch fabrics can create an attractive smocked effect.

For free-motion stitching with a foot

The same considerations as for free-motion embroidery without a foot apply to free-motion stitching with an embroidery or darning foot. The only difference is that because the foot holds the fabric firmly for the needle to enter, it does not need to be stretched as tightly.

If the fabric is firm, or backed with interfacing or some sort of stabilizer (see opposite), it should be possible to hold it by hand rather than stretching it in a hoop. Read through the different techniques detailed on pages 44–45 and 50–51, and decide which method is most suitable for your chosen fabric.

Lining and backing

Using a lining, interfacing, or other backing fabric will alter the working quality of a fabric, making it possible to machine embroider difficult fabrics and changing the character of some fabrics to give them quite different stitching effects. Any firmly woven fabric can be used as a backing, but there is also a whole range of special fabrics that can be very useful.

Batting

Polyester batting is available in light, medium, and heavy weights, all of which are suitable to use for incorporating into a machine stitched project. The medium weight is probably most suitable for quilting, since it will give a pleasant raised effect to the quilted areas but will also remain flexible and therefore drape well. Wool and cotton battings are also available; they are warmer but give a flatter, less raised appearance to the finished quilt.

Interfacing

Interfacing comes in light, medium, and heavy weights.
• Fusible interfacing has an adhesive side that will adhere firmly to the fabric when ironed; it forms a very good bond and a firm foundation for stitching, but also alters the character of the fabric, making it much less pliable.
• Sew-in interfacing is more suitable for adding body without altering the appearance of the fabric. The fabric is pinned or basted securely over the interfacing, and the two layers are then treated as one when being stitched.
• Valance interfacing is particularly firm and, although easy to stitch through, will create a stiff effect (see the Decorated Box on pages 46–49).

Fusible web

Double-sided fusible interfacing, or fusible web, will fix one fabric to another and is ideal for appliqué projects or for creating layers of sheer fabrics with stitching details between them (see the Table Settings on pages 94–96). A fusible hemming tape is also available and is useful for bonding the folded-under edges of a stitched picture.

Stabilizer

A stabilizer is a non-woven material similar to interfacing and is used under a fine fabric to give it sufficient body for decorative stitching. Some types are pinned or basted in place, others are slightly adhesive. After embroidering, the stabilizer can be torn away easily from around the stitching.

Vanishing fabric

Vanishing fabrics were developed to create a surface on which to work machine embroidery. Lines of stitches are worked to form an interconnecting net, which can then be embroidered further to create either a lacy or a densely woven effect. When stitching is complete, the vanishing fabric is dissolved or pulled away by various methods. For guidance on using vanishing fabrics, see pages 80–81.

Threads

The main difference between sewing and embroidery threads lies in their thicknesses and strength. Mercerized sewing thread is twisted tightly and then treated chemically to make it stronger. This step is necessary for seaming but not for decoration. Embroidery threads are finer, which means that there is much more on a spool and when working blocks of color the fibers spread out to create a denser mass.

Both types of thread offer a range of colors, but many more variegated and metallic effects are available in embroidery thread. Machine embroidery threads are available in a wide variety of natural and synthetic fibers, in matt or luster finishes. Threads with a mixture of natural and synthetic fibers will be stronger.

15

hoops & other equipment

Other than a sewing machine, the only other essential piece of equipment for machine embroidery, particularly free-motion embroidery, is an embroidery hoop or frame. Hoops are widely available from notions department and craft stores, but since they are also used for hand embroidery, you may already have one. Similarly, you will probably already have many of the other items listed here as part of your general sewing equipment.

Embroidery hoops

Embroidery hoops and frames may be made from plastic, wood, or metal and are available in a range of sizes. They are usually circular but may also be rectangular.

For most machine-embroidery purposes, you should choose a circular wooden hoop with a fixing screw to tighten it, since this type will hold the fabric most securely. The hoop should be somewhere between 5" (12cm) and 8" (20cm) in diameter and no more than ¼" (6mm) thick so that it can slide easily under the needle. If a wooden hoop is thicker, saw a small cut part-way through one side through which to slide the needle.

A spring-loaded plastic hoop is useful for working on very lightweight fabrics that tear easily, because it will not grip the fabric so tightly.

Binding a hoop

If a wooden hoop does not hold the fabric taut, or the fabric slips during stitching, the grip can be improved by binding the inner hoop with a cotton twill tape or by gluing narrow velvet ribbon around the outside of it.

To bind the hoop with tape, secure one end of the tape to the inner hoop using a spot of all-purpose glue. Bind the tape diagonally around the hoop, stretching it tightly while wrapping and overlapping the preceding edge at each turn. Fix the end with another spot of glue, and allow the glue to dry before using the hoop.

To bind with velvet ribbon, choose a ribbon that is no wider than the hoop. Follow the instructions above, gluing a single layer of ribbon around the outside of the inner hoop and butting the ends together neatly. Allow the glue to dry completely before using the hoop.

Mounting fabric in a hoop

1 Place the outer hoop on a clean, flat surface. Then lay the fabric right side up over the hoop making sure that the design is centered.

2 Press the inner hoop into the outer one, and gently pull the fabric all around to make a taut drum.

3 Push down the inner ring firmly so that the fabric is held quite flat against the surface, and tighten the fixing screw. The inner ring should protrude slightly below the outer ring.

General equipment

To make any of the projects in the book or to experiment with the different stitching techniques, it would be useful to have the following equipment or accessories readily available for each embroidery session.

Scissors

Use dressmaker's scissors for cutting fabric, household scissors for cutting paper patterns, and small, sharp scissors for trimming threads, removing unwanted thread, and for cutting away threads jammed in the shuttle race.

Seam ripper or unpicker

These are used for slashing through layered fabrics, cutting through satin-stitch loops to create fringed effects, and for removing misplaced stitches.

Tape measure

A tape measure or long ruler is essential for measuring fabric lengths.

Pins

Sharp dressmaker's pins are essential for most machine-embroidery projects.

Hand-sewing needles

Most of the projects in the book require some hand finishing, so a selection of these, including a tapestry needle and a bodkin, is useful.

Needlecase

Keep all your needles, including any machine needles reserved for particular threads, in a needlecase (see page 23). Hand stitch a length of the appropriate thread next to each needle's position for reference if desired.

Bobbins

It is very useful to have extra bobbins so that each thread is instantly available without having to wind one color over another or throw away thread to make a bobbin available. Store bobbins in a divided bobbin box so that they are visible and remain neatly wound.

Bobbin case

If your work frequently uses altered bobbin tension techniques (see pages 92–93) and you use a machine with a vertical bobbin case (see page 11), it is useful to have one bobbin case permanently set to a normal tension and a second bobbin case set to a loose tension. Mark one with a spot of nail polish to distinguish them.

Needle guard

If the correct hand position is used on a hoop or to grip the fabric, it is very unlikely that the needle will come into contact with your hand. However, this is a common worry, and some machine manufacturers make and sell a clear plastic needle guard as an accessory.

Pencils and markers

Most projects will require a pattern or outline to be marked on the fabric before stitching. You should use either a very sharp, hard pencil or a special marker (see page 18).

Other drawing tools

A straight-edged ruler, pair of compasses, and a draftsman's triangle are useful for accurate marking.

preparation & aftercare

Whether you use the patterns and designs in this book, find motifs from other sources, or draw your own sketches on paper, you will need to transfer the designs onto the fabric before stitching. To make most of the projects in this book, the design outlines will need to be enlarged before transferring, and this may apply to other artwork as well. Finally, the finished embroidery may have become unacceptably distorted and will need to be stretched back into shape.

Enlarging designs

Most of the designs and patterns in this book cannot be shown actual size because of space limitations. Similarly, designs taken from other sources may need to be enlarged or reduced before they are stitched. OR REDUCING

The simplest method of enlarging a design is to use a photocopier. The design outlines in this book that require enlarging each have the correct percentage enlargement noted beside them. For other designs you might wish to embroider, work out the required finished size (height and width), take it with the design to a photocopy shop, and ask for help in working out the percentage.

Transferring designs

For all but the simplest lines of decorative stitching, you will need to transfer the outlines of a design onto the fabric before stitching. Your choice of marker will be influenced by the stitching. Will the stitches be worked in fine lines, as on the Decorated Box on pages 46–49, or will they cover the background and hide all the lines, as in the Lying on a Rug picture on pages 66–69? Also consider whether the finished article will need to be washed or not. Whatever marker you choose, try it out on a scrap of fabric first to see how obvious it is, whether it smudges, and whether it will be possible to remove it if necessary.

Markers

• For lines that may not be hidden completely by the stitching, use a very sharp, hard pencil, and make the lines as fine as possible.

• Alternatively, use a water-soluble marking pen or a vanishing pen, available from needlecraft stores and notions departments; these make lines that can be removed.

Water-soluble pen marks disappear when sprayed with water, but make sure your fabric and threads are colorfast. Vanishing pens work very well on some fabrics and not on others. The line should fade after two or three days, but sometimes the line appears to fade and then it reappears some days later!

For both types of marking pen, do not iron the fabric while the lines are still visible, as this will fix them permanently.

• Tailor's chalk is the traditional marker and, if it has a sharp edge, makes a good removable line for quick stitching, but it would wear off or smudge if used to draw the outlines of an intricate design.

• Design lines that will eventually be hidden can be marked in pencil or with a permanent, fine felt-tipped pen if a more obvious line is preferred.

• For marking lines on vanishing fabric, use a permanent, fine felt-tipped pen.

Transferring methods

There are several different methods of transferring a machine-embroidery design from paper to fabric.

• Lay the fabric over the outline, place both on a light box, and simply trace the lines. A similar technique is to pin the fabric over the outline, and tape both to a large windowpane.

• Place a piece of dressmaker's carbon paper (tracing paper) over the fabric, with the design outline on top of that, then carefully draw over the outline, using a sharp pencil.

• Use the old-fashioned method of tracing the outline, turning the tracing paper over and drawing over the lines using a sharp, soft pencil. Then lay the tracing the right way up on the fabric, and draw over the lines again. The outline will be transferred onto the fabric and can be redefined using a hard pencil or permanent felt-tipped pen.

• Alternatively, draw on the back of the tracing using a special transfer pencil, then apply the image to the fabric by pressing with a warm iron.

• For simple shapes, such as the roof pieces of the Decorated Box on pages 46–49 or the circles in the Button Collection on pages 62–63 or for a motif that will be used repeatedly, cut out the shape from thin cardboard, and use it as a template.

Aftercare

Both hand and machine embroidering frequently tend to distort the shape of the fabric. An uneven surface texture may add to the character of the design, but if a wavy outline or undulating surface detracts from the finished effect, the embroidery can be pressed or stretched to reduce the distortion.

fig 1

Pressing

Before pressing a machine-embroidered piece, consider carefully whether it is really necessary. If the fabric has been pressed before stretching in a hoop, the embroidered area should not need pressing afterward.

Pieces stitched with ordinary mercerized sewing thread will respond well to pressing, and most machine-embroidery threads will withstand hot temperatures – except the metallic threads, which should be pressed with a cool iron and caution. Pressing any embroidery obviously flattens the stitches, and this can detract from the finished effect.

If you need to press an embroidered piece and do not want to flatten the stitches, lay the embroidery right side down on a bath towel, and press the back of the work lightly, using a steam iron and avoiding any downward pressure on the iron.

Stretching

To stretch machine embroidery, you will need a piece of plywood or fiberboard at least ⅜" (1cm) thick and larger than the finished design, a similarly sized old blanket or towel, a water spray, and rustproof tacks.

1 Lay the blanket or towel over the board, and dampen it by spraying.
2 Lay the embroidery on top, and spray lightly with water. Most thread and fabric colors will be colorfast with a light spray, but check the fastness of any hand-dyed threads or fabrics.
3 Secure the embroidery in the center of each side with a tack, stretching the work slightly between the tacks.
4 Working on alternate sides and away from each central tack, stretch and tack the sides until the tacks meet at the corners and the embroidery is flat (fig 1).
5 Leave until thoroughly dry, then unpin. Do not try to speed up drying by placing the work near direct heat.

Set-stitch decoration

The simplest piece of topstitching along a seam or a satin-stitch edging on a pillowcase qualifies as machine embroidery. Whereas the techniques for embroidering or embellishing by hand are different from those used for stitching an item together, exactly the same machine-stitching techniques can be used for utility or for decorative work.

Creating an ornamental effect by machine can be as simple as stitching a single line. For the first forays into machine embroidery, as illustrated by the projects in this chapter, there is no need to adjust the machine settings – a whole variety of attractive effects can be achieved simply by threading your machine and starting to stitch. The decoration is created by choosing effective combinations of thread colors, experimenting with those little-used attachments provided with most machines, pressing and pleating the fabric, or by quilting it subtly to create softly padded relief patterns.

beginning steps

Using a sewing machine for embroidery need not require learning any new techniques or skills – just working lines of contrasting colored stitching across a piece of plain fabric can be all the decoration that is needed to transform a simple design into a decorative piece. Stitching embellishment on the fabric in this way, rather than using the machine for seaming pieces together, is also a useful introduction to working on all parts of a piece of fabric rather than just around the edges.

Setting up the machine

The four projects in this chapter all require the sewing machine to be set up for normal stitching. If the machine is unfamiliar to you, consult the manual for advice on inserting the bobbin, how to thread, and other general instructions, but even if the machine is one you have used a lot for general sewing, it is worth spending some time cleaning and adjusting the machine to achieve the best possible performance for embroidery (see Problem Solving opposite).

Starting to stitch

It is always a good idea to work some sample stitching on fabric scraps, but when the stitching is decorative, it is even more important to work a test piece first, using the fabric, interfacing or batting, and threads that are to be used for the actual piece.

Hold the threads out of the way at the start of stitching so that they do not tangle, and get used to finishing stitching with the thread take-up lever at the highest point so that when stitching is started again the top thread is not pulled out of the needle. Start and finish every line of stitching with a few backstitches to secure the ends.

Straight stitch

1 Sew a few lines of straight stitch, and remove the test piece from the machine.
2 First, check that the tension is correctly adjusted (see page 11); if necessary, use a different-colored needle thread for further test stitching so that tension faults are more obvious.
3 Then consider the stitch length: a 3mm stitch length is average for embroidery (about eight stitches per inch), but fine fabrics will need a shorter than average stitch-length setting and heavy fabrics a longer one. The length chosen should glide across the work without causing it to pucker. As a general guide, on lightweight fabrics choose a slightly shorter stitch-length setting for decorative stitching than for seaming.

Zigzag and satin stitch

Satin stitch is simply zigzag stitch worked with a very short stitch-length setting so that the stitches are close enough together to form a solid bar. All machines will have a variety of stitch-width settings; some will move up in steps, while others will be graduated.

Any tension problems will be much more obvious with zigzag or satin stitch and may cause pinching or puckering of the fabric. If the bobbin thread appears on the top side (below left), loosen the needle-thread tension slightly. If the needle thread is being pulled under (below right), tighten the needle-thread tension. With perfect tension, the threads are drawn equally into the fabric (see page 11).

Decorative techniques

The methods of stitching are no different than those used for ordinary sewing, but because the stitching is intended as decoration it will be more visible. To enhance the decorative effect, try backing the fabric with interfacing (see page 15), which will quilt the fabric slightly, creating a carved, raised effect.

From the top: short straight stitch, triple stitch, zigzag stitch, satin stitch, satin stitch ribbon, a utility stitch pattern

Straight-stitch effects

• For a small piece of work, such as the silk bags on pages 24–27, a short stitch length (with the tension properly adjusted) will create a slightly raised line of stitching – working such short stitches on a larger piece could be tedious!

• When straight stitching small grids, try using the backstitch setting for alternate lines of stitching.

• Some machines have a triple-stitch facility, which works three stitches at every stitch position. A similar effect can be achieved by stitching carefully over a line of stitching so that the needle enters the original holes.

• To create defined corners, always pivot stitching lines with the needle through the fabric. Remember to raise the presser bar before pivoting and lower it before you resume stitching.

• For narrow parallel lines, stitch with one side of the machine foot alongside the first row of stitching. For wider parallel lines, use a quilting bar or measuring arm, which screws into the back of the machine foot (see your sewing machine manual) and can be fixed so that one end rests on the first line of stitching.

Zigzag and other stitch effects

• Experiment with different length and width settings for zigzag and satin stitch.

• Practice satin stitching to achieve the closest setting possible. Start with a 1mm stitch length and gradually shorten it: too close and the machine will begin to make some stitches over others, creating an uneven finished effect.

• Alter the width setting while the machine is stitching satin stitch, to create graduated ribbons of stitching.

• Loosen the needle-thread tension very slightly for satin stitch embroidery, to create a rounded bar effect rather than flat stitching.

• When making zigzag or satin-stitch corners, the position of the needle is important. If it is at the inside point of the corner when the fabric is pivoted, the result will be an open corner. If it is at the outside point, the corner will be closed and more angular.

• Practice stitching satin-stitch curves with an embroidery foot. To stitch perfect circles, draw them around a template or using a compass, and stitch carefully over the lines. Alternatively, try taping a thumbtack to the needle plate, with the point through the tape. Push the fabric onto the pin, and stitch – the fabric will automatically be fed in a circle. Changing the position of the pin will change the circle size.

• Try out any other utility stitch patterns the machine can produce, such as shell stitch, blind stitch, or scallops.

Open corner

Closed corner

Problem solving

• Damaged needles are the most common cause of skipped stitches or poor stitching. A bent needle may hit the needle plate, which could then tear or pull on the fabric.

• Every thread wears a different groove in a new needle, and using one needle for different threads may cause thread breakages. If you have this problem, try keeping a needle for each thread type.

• Clean your sewing machine regularly, brushing out fluff and lint around the feed, shuttle race, and needle bar.

• An unevenly wound bobbin may cause irregular stitching. If the loaded bobbin does not resemble a neat spool, rewind.

• Check that the machine is correctly threaded – there may be a thread guide that is easy to overlook but which, if used, will enhance the stitching.

bags of style

Three silk bags enhanced with lines of stitching show just how simple it is to develop straight stitching into a decorative effect. The embellishment on the bags is created with combinations of straight, blind, and satin stitches, often using a measuring arm, quilting bar, or the side of the foot to work parallel lines of stitching to form different grid effects. Choose a limited range of thread colors, including repeats of the fabric shades.

   The bags illustrated are self-lined with silk to use as evening or jewelry bags, but the two larger ones could also be lined with shower-curtain fabric to make deliciously decadent yet practical make-up bags.

Stitch methods

Set straight stitch
Set satin stitch
Set blind stitch
Tension: normal settings throughout

Feet: normal presser foot, plus
   measuring arm or quilter foot with
   quilting bar, if available
Needle: 12/80

Ring bag

You will need

2 pieces slubbed silk, each 8" x 12" (20 x 30cm), in contrasting colors
8" x 12" (20 x 30cm) sew-in medium-weight interfacing
Sewing thread in 2 contrasting colors
Sewing thread to match lining
1¼ yd (1m) cord
Eyelet punch and eyelets (optional)

To prepare the fabric

1 Enlarge pattern piece to 156%, then to 156% on a photocopier, and add a ⅜" (1cm) seam allowance all around.
2 Cut out 2 bag pieces from each color of silk, and lay aside the two lining pieces. Cut out 2 bag pieces from interfacing. Press all pieces.
3 Back each bag piece that is to be embroidered with an interfacing piece, pinning or basting layers together.

To work the embroidery

Work decorative lines of stitching to raw edges when appropriate, securing at each end. Back of bag has a simple grid with short bars of satin-stitch detail; front has horizontal lines of straight stitch and a satin-stitch cross in center of the bag, with circles of stitching radiating around it.

To make the bag

1 Lay each embroidered bag piece right sides together with a lining piece, and stitch all around with a ⅜" (1cm) seam allowance, leaving a small gap to turn through. Trim, turn right side out, and hand stitch gap closed. Press.
2 At narrowest part of neck, mark 2 eyelet holes on each bag piece as indicated on pattern piece. Either use an eyelet punch to secure an eyelet in each, or work small buttonholes.
3 Lay embroidered sides of bag pieces together, and stitch circular body parts together with a ⅛" (3mm) seam allowance. Turn bag right side out, and press. Thread cord twice around bag through eyelets or buttonholes.

Enlarge to 156% and then to 156% on a photocopier and add ⅜" (1cm) seam allowance all around.

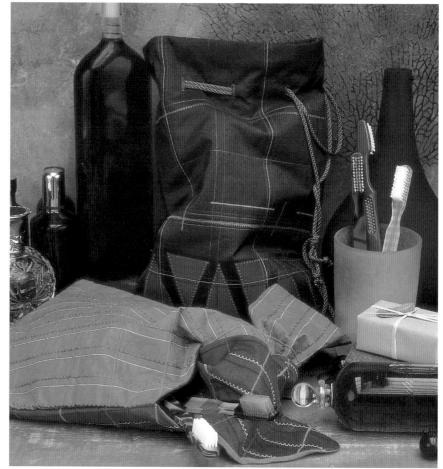

Enlarge to the measurements shown and add a
⅜" (1cm) seam allowance all around.

4¼"
(10cm)

14¼"
(36cm)

Tie bag

9"
(23cm)

10¼" (26cm)

You will need

2 pieces slubbed silk, each 25½" x 24"
(65 x 60cm), in contrasting colors
25½" x 24" (65 x 60cm) sew-in medium-
weight interfacing
Sewing thread in 2 matching and
2 contrasting colors

To prepare the fabric

1 Enlarge pattern piece on the left to the
measurements shown.
2 Cut out 2 bag pieces from each color
of silk, and lay aside one of each color
to use for making the lining. Cut out 2
bag pieces from sew-in interfacing.
Press all pieces.
3 Back each bag piece that is to be
embroidered with an interfacing piece,
pinning or basting layers together
securely so that they do not slip.

To work the embroidery

Work a stitched grid over each bag
piece, using the photograph above as a
guide for the grid. Use the matching
sewing thread colors for satin-stitch lines
and contrasting colors for utility or
zigzag lines.

To make the bag

1 Lay each embroidered bag piece right
sides together with a contrasting lining
piece, and stitch all around with a ⅜"
(1cm) seam allowance, leaving a small
gap to turn through. Trim, turn right side
out, and hand stitch gap closed. Press.
2 Lay embroidered sides of bag pieces
together, and stitch sides and base
together with a ¼" (6mm) seam
allowance, finishing securely at both
ends. Turn bag right side out, and press.

Rectangular bag

You will need

26" x 19¼" (66 x 49cm) slubbed silk
Contrasting slubbed silk scraps
26" x 19¼" (66 x 49cm) sew-in medium-
    weight interfacing
4" x 12" (10 x 30cm) fusible web
Sewing thread in 2 matching and
    2 contrasting colors
2¼yd (2m) cord
Eyelet punch and eyelets (optional)

To prepare the fabric

1 Press rectangular silk and interfacing pieces, then back silk piece with interfacing, basting layers together.
2 Back scraps of contrasting silk with fusible web following manufacturer's instructions, and cut out 13 triangles, using template below.
3 Lay triangles along one short edge of rectangle (fig 1), with bases about 1½" (4cm) from rectangle edge and outside points of end triangles about ¾" (2cm) from rectangle sides. Fuse in place.

To work the embroidery

Work a simple linear grid of straight stitch, zigzag stitch, and satin stitch over the rectangle, as shown in the photograph on page 26. Continue lengthwise stitching lines across the lining half, but work shorter, widthwise stitching lines and satin-stitch bars on the outer, appliquéd half only. Continue all the lines of stitching to raw edges, and secure at both ends.

To make the bag

1 With right sides together, fold embroidered rectangle in half widthwise, and stitch together around raw edges with a ⅜" (1cm) seam allowance, but leaving a small gap to turn through. Trim, turn right side out, and hand stitch gap closed.
2 Measure 2" (5cm) down from folded edge, and mark 8 evenly spaced eyelet points for cord. Either use an eyelet punch to secure an eyelet in each, or work small buttonholes.
3 With right sides together, fold bag in half widthwise, and stitch side and base together with a ¼" (6mm) seam allowance. Turn bag right side out, and press. Thread cord twice around bag through eyelets or buttonholes (fig 2).

triangle template

fig 1

fig 2

unusual feet & needles

Even the oldest treadle sewing machine came with a box of specialized feet and attachments. Modern machines have a whole variety of attachments and programs designed to make home sewing easier and more professional, but although the wide range of applications might have been an important selling point, once home they can easily be forgotten. So, spend some time sorting out the attachments to your machine, then stitch some samples to remind yourself of their decorative potential.

Tailor-tacking foot

The tailor-tacking foot (see page 12) has a raised bar in the center and is used with zigzag stitch. The needle-thread tension is loosened slightly to allow each top stitch to form into a loop.

This foot can be used to form fringes or to make a line of faggoting. For a fringe, set the stitch length to 1mm or less and the width as wide as possible, and work a line of satin stitch. The stitches can be left as a looped fringe or trimmed.

The stitches are not secured into the fabric, so they must be fixed in some way. Either fuse a strip of iron-on interfacing to the wrong side of the fabric, or when the line of fringe has been stitched, replace the normal presser foot, retighten the tension, and holding the fringe to one side with your finger, work a row of narrow satin stitch over the base of the loops.

Faggoting

Faggoting is a method of joining two pieces of fabric with a delicate line of stitches and holes, and is often seen as hand-worked embroidery on old linen towels and pillowcases.

1 Lay two pieces of fabric right sides together, with the raw edges zigzagged and lying even, and stitch the seam with a ¼" (6mm) seam allowance (fig 1).

2 Gently pull the layers of fabric apart, and press the seam allowances open (fig 2). Replace the normal presser foot, retighten the tension, and stitch along the folded fabric edge on either side of the faggoting with a narrow satin stitch.

Alternative faggoting techniques

It is possible to work faggoting without a tailor-tacking foot on a machine with a faggoting stitch or with a 3-step zigzag utility pattern.

1 Trim the seam allowances to ¼" (6mm) and zigzag the raw edges, then press to the wrong side to make crisp folds.

2 Baste one folded edge to a strip of tear-away stabilizer. Measure exactly ⅛" (3mm) across the stabilizer, and baste the second folded edge in place.

3 Center the machine foot over the gap, and stitch along it so that alternate edges are caught in the stitching. Tear away the stabilizer.

fig 1

fig 2

Twin needles

The effect of twin-needle stitching is to create slightly raised pintucks that are much finer than pleated pintucks. Most swing-needle machines can be fitted with a twin needle for straight stitching, while some can also use one on a zigzag setting narrow enough that the needle will not hit the needle plate. There are a variety of sizes of twin needles available (see page 12), and they can be used with a normal sewing machine presser foot or with a grooved pintuck foot, which is useful for sewing exactly parallel rows of fine pintucks.

• Follow the instructions in the manual for threading your machine for twin-needle stitching. The threads are initially threaded together but are separated at the tension disk or lowest thread guide.

A single bobbin thread is used.
• The rows of pintucks created by twin-needle stitching can be worked in a self color for a subtle effect or with two slightly different shades of thread.

Wing needle

Wing needles are used to replicate traditional hand hemstitching, in which threads are withdrawn from linen handkerchiefs or bed linen and the resulting holes embellished with hand stitching. Wing needles work by pushing the threads apart to form a hole. They are available in standard needle sizes and also as twin needles, which actually have one wing needle with a standard needle on the same shank.

• A successful result with wing-needle stitching depends largely on the choice of fabric. Crisp, natural fabrics work best: the fabric must have a loose enough weave for the wing needle to push the threads apart rather than cutting or pulling them, and it must be firm enough to retain the hole once the needle has been withdrawn.

• Prepare fabrics for wing-needle stitching by spraying with spray starch and pressing them well.
• Experiment with stitching more than once into the holes to increase the effect, or try zigzag (using a single wing needle only). Alternatively, tighten the needle-thread tension slightly to increase the size of the holes created.

Problem solving

• For a successful result when working zigzag stitching with a twin needle, it may help to loosen the bobbin tension slightly (see page 11).

• Using an open-toe presser foot rather than a normal presser foot makes it easier to see what is happening when working a decorative stitch effect.

crib quilt

Log-cabin quilting, with a central square surrounded by increasingly long strips of fabric, is a traditional patchwork method. It is an ideal way to use old household linen and to try out a variety of stitches and new techniques.

Old-fashioned dishtowels, damask table linen, linen sheets, huck towels, and any other washable fabrics of a similar weight are ideal. Work sampler center squares of all the decorative stitch patterns that your sewing machine produces, then search through the attachment box, and try out the tailor-tacking foot and any other little-used devices. Surround the squares with strips of the same fabric, then either stitch them into a delightful baby's crib quilt or make them into a bolster, pillow cover, or curtain.

Stitch methods

Set straight stitch
Set satin stitch
Set utility stitches
Tension: normal settings throughout
Feet: normal presser foot, open-toe
     presser foot, tailor-tacking foot
Needles: 12/80; wing needle, twin
     needle (optional)

You will need

For a crib quilt measuring 33" x 24"
(84 x 60cm):
1¾yd (1.5m) in total of assorted
     lightweight fabrics, 36" (90cm) or
     44" (112cm) wide
28" x 39" (70 x 100cm) warm backing
     fabric
3½yd (3m) satin ribbon, 1½" (4cm) wide
Sewing threads in assorted colors, for
     decoration
White sewing thread, for sewing pieces
     together
Assorted linen buttons, cotton tape,
     name tapes, lace, and ribbon
Rotary cutter and board (optional)

To cut out

1 Each finished log-cabin block measures 4¾" (12cm) square. For each square, you will need to cut out a 2⅛" (5.5cm) central square and long strips of fabric, each ⅞" (2cm) wide. These must be accurate so that finished blocks are all exactly the same size. Using pencil and ruler, mark cutting lines lightly on the wrong side of the fabric.

2 Using rotary cutter and board (the easiest and most accurate method of cutting a number of layers), cut out 35 central squares and a mass of strips for a quilt cover. Each block requires approximately 2¼yd (2m) of strips, which can be any length from 2⅛" (5.5cm) to full width of fabric.

To embroider the central squares

Use central squares to try out effects of different stitching patterns: straight stitch, different widths of zigzag and satin stitch, and any utility or decorative stitch pattern available on your machine. Make buttonholes on some, and use a button attachment to sew on old linen buttons. (**Note:** Buttons on a baby's quilt should be attached *very* securely.)

Try faggoting with a tailor-tacking foot, or experiment with a wing needle on a crisp linen square. Other squares could have ribbons or rows of tape laid across them. (**Note:** Again, on a baby's quilt insure that they are stitched on securely.) Some damask or huck-towel squares can be left plain.

To work a log-cabin block

1 Lay a central square and a fabric strip right sides together, with one end of fabric strip even with edge of square (fig 1). Cut other end of strip even with opposite edge of square. Stitch square to strip with a ¼in (5mm) seam allowance, securing at both ends (it is vital that you use accurate seam allowances). Then press the stitched seam open.

2 Turn square through 90°, and apply a second strip of same fabric as before (fig 2). Press seam open.

3 Turn square as before, and apply a third strip in same manner, then repeat once more so that central square is completely enclosed by the strips (fig 3).

4 Using either same or different fabric, repeat steps 1–3 to enclose square again. Continue to add fabric strips until each side of central square has 4 strips stitched around it.

fig 1

fig 2

fig 3

To make the quilt

1 Make 35 blocks, trim any that are slightly big or uneven, and arrange to form a pleasing design 5 squares wide by 7 squares long.

2 Sew first row of 7 squares together with ¼" (5mm) seam allowances. Repeat for remaining 4 rows of 7 squares. Press all seams open, join rows together, and press seams open.

3 Trim backing fabric to same size as patchwork, place wrong sides together, and pin all around. Lay right side of satin ribbon along one edge of quilt with edges even, and stitch with a ⅜" (1cm) seam allowance. Miter ribbon at corners (fig 4), and fold final end of ribbon under to make a neat join.

4 Fold ribbon to underside of cover, and slipstitch edge in place by hand.

fig 4

pleating & quilting

Machine embroidery is often used to apply surface decoration to a piece of fabric, but there are a wide variety of attractive effects to be created by altering the character of the fabric through padding or pleating. Lines of stitching can be used to form the fabric into crisp tucks or pleats, softly quilted layers, or neat channels. The choice of thread color will determine whether the stitching lines are a discreet part of the overall effect or a distinctive embellishment.

Pleating

A variety of effects can be created by pleating and stitching from the subtle lines of twin-needle pintucks to deep furrows of folded fabric. Once the initial pleating is complete, it can be topstitched or formed into waves by cross stitching. To form precise pleats, spend time on the preparation, measuring and marking carefully, and the actual stitching will be simple to work.

Plain pleats

Pleating uses a surprising amount of fabric: allow 2½–3 times the finished length, or carefully calculate the fabric quantities. It may help to draw the pleating pattern on plain or graph paper.
1 Work out the required depth of pleats, taking into consideration the weight of the fabric – a thick fabric will be too bulky for fine pleats. Then decide on the distance between them (placement area). When working out the fabric quantity err on the generous side, as all the folding and stitching tends to reduce both the width and the expected length.
2 Cut out a rectangle of fabric, insuring that the corners are square, and lay it right side up on a clean, hard surface. Using a long ruler and sharp, very hard pencil, draw a line across the width of the fabric a short way from the edge and parallel to it. Using a draftsman's triangle against the ruler for accuracy, measure the pleat's finished width down from the first line and draw a parallel line, then repeat: when folded along the center one, these three lines will form the first pleat. Measure the placement area width from the last line, and draw another block of three lines. Continue to measure and mark to the other end of the fabric (fig 1).
3 Thread your sewing machine with matching needle and bobbin threads,

and set to straight stitch and a 2.5mm to 3mm stitch length. Fold and press the first pleat, then stitch directly along the marked line to secure it. Continue to fold, press, and stitch the pleats in the same way to the end of the fabric.

Cross-stitched pleats

1 Measure along the completed plain pleats, and divide the fabric into even sections, adding a generous trimming allowance at each side.
2 Using a quilting bar or a measuring arm (see page 23) to insure straight lines, stitch across the pleats from alternate marked points.
3 Turn the fabric 180°, and stitch straight lines back across the pleats halfway between each original line of stitching, insuring that the pleats lie in opposite directions to create a wave effect (fig 2).

Contrast topstitching

1 Before cross stitching the pleats, thread your machine with contrasting needle and bobbin threads. Test the tension on a fabric scrap: it should be as near perfect as possible (see page 11).
2 Stitch three evenly spaced rows along the length of each pleat, making sure that the same color is always on top.
3 Replace the contrasting thread with the self color before cross stitching.

pleat width

placement area

pleat

pleat

fig 1

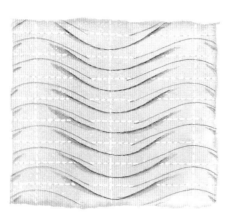

fig 2

Quilting

All sorts of quilting effects can be created quickly by machine. Spaghetti, or Italian, quilting is stitched first and filled afterward. Another effect, similar to trapunto, or stuffed work, can be created easily using batting and machine stitching.

Spaghetti quilting

Spaghetti quilting is formed by stitching narrow channels on a transparent silk fabric and then threading knitting yarn or needlepoint tapestry yarn through them. It is a delightful effect, which can be enhanced by using colored wool yarns that create softly muted shades when seen through the lightweight silk, and by stitching the channels with a twin machine needle.

Choose a very fine, white or ivory transparent silk, and the same quantity of white muslin. Allow about 2" (5cm) extra on each side, since the technique will reduce the fabric area.

1 Lay the silk right side up over the muslin, and starting in the center, baste the layers together (fig 3). Using tailor's chalk and a ruler, draw a line across the top of the fabric parallel to the edge.

2 Set up the machine up for twin-needle stitching (see page 29), and stitch over the chalk line. Using the outside of the foot as a width guide, stitch a second line parallel to the first (fig 4). Continue until all the fabric is stitched into evenly spaced channels.

3 Thread a blunt-ended tapestry needle with two lengths of tapestry yarn used double, and working from the muslin side, thread it into a channel and work the needle along to the end. Thread all the channels with yarn in the same way.

The yarn colors will change considerably when seen through the silk, so take the fabric with you to hold over the yarn when choosing shades.

fig 3

fig 4

Trapunto quilting

True trapunto quilting, or stuffed work, is formed by laying one fabric over a backing fabric, stitching outline shapes to form contained areas, then cutting through the backing fabric and stuffing each outline separately. Alternatively, it can be worked by placing stuffing under appliqué patches and sewing them onto the fabric.

A similar effect, which is better suited to machine embroidery, can be created using a printed fabric with a pattern composed of fairly bold outline shapes.

1 Make a quilting sandwich of backing fabric (right side down), stuffing or batting, and top fabric (right side up), and pin the layers together.

2 Starting in the middle, baste the layers together (see fig 3 left). It is important that the layers are not able to move independently of each other, or the finished effect may be marred by tucks stitched on the underside. On a large piece of work, you may also need to baste lines parallel to the fabric edges.

3 Set your machine for straight stitch, with a stitch length of about 3mm. Choose needle threads to match the areas of the printed design, and use a bobbin thread to match the backing fabric throughout. Stitch around some motifs, working the amount of quilting to suit the fabric design – a neat repeating pattern will be enhanced by regular quilting, while a more abstract design can have fairly random quilting.

pleated & pressed pillows

A combination of natural colors and precisely stitched pleats and channels creates a collection of pillows that are simply satisfying. A limited number of fabrics and colors were chosen, and these are combined to make individually attractive pillows that also work together as a pleasing group. The decorative stitching could not be simpler – on each pillow the effect is created by parallel lines of straight stitching, the secret of success is to measure and mark out the stitching lines accurately and to stitch precisely so that all the pleats or channels are exactly the same width.

Spaghetti-quilted pillow

fig 1

Stitch methods
Set straight stitch
Tension: normal settings throughout
Feet: normal presser foot, zipper foot
Needles: 1.6/70 twin needle, 12/80
    ordinary needle

You will need
For a pillow 16" (40cm) square:
20" (50cm) square transparent silk
20" (50cm) square muslin
17" x 36" (43 x 90cm) backing fabric
Ivory sewing thread
12 11yd (10m) skeins tapestry yarn
    (3 skeins each of 4 colors)
2yd (1.8m) fine filler cord
12" (30cm) zipper
Pillow form to fit cover
Blunt-ended tapestry needle

To work spaghetti quilting
1 Following instructions on page 35, lay transparent silk square over muslin square, and baste together. Using tailor's chalk, draw a fine line across center of square. Thread machine with ivory sewing thread, and using a twin needle, stitch along marked line. Using machine foot as a width guide, cover square with equally spaced narrow channels.
2 Remove all basting threads. Thread tapestry needle with 2 38" (96cm) lengths of tapestry yarn used double to create 4 strands, and work needle though first channel. Cut off yarn. Using 4 yarn colors in rotation, thread all channels in the same way (fig 1).
3 Using a long ruler, draftsman's triangle, and tailor's chalk, mark stitching lines at right angles to channels. Using normal single needle, stitch parallel lines of stitching across spaghetti quilting.

To trim the quilted square
1 Trim quilted square and backing fabric to 17" (43cm) square.
2 Cut extra backing fabric into bias strips 1½" (4cm) wide. Join to form a strip 2yd (1.8m) long, and use to cover cord. Trim seam allowance to ½" (12mm).
3 Pin piping all around quilted square. Stitch along stitching line on piping, using a zipper foot.

To make the pillow cover
Make pillow cover, leaving a ½" (12mm) seam allowance and inserting zipper along one side. Insert pillow form.

Natural pleated pillow

Stitch methods

Set straight stitch
Tension: normal settings throughout
Feet: normal presser foot, zipper foot
Needle: 12/80

You will need

For a pillow 18" (45cm) square:
28" x 31" (71 x 79cm) rough silk
Light and dark contrasting sewing
    threads
2¼ yd (2m) fringed edging
14" (35cm) zipper
Pillow form to fit cover

To cut out

Follow cutting layout in fig 1, and cut
1 pillow back, 2 short front panels, and 1
long front panel to be pleated.

fig 1

fig 2

 ¼" (2cm)

To work the pleated panel

1 Press long front panel, and using a
ruler and draftsman's triangle, draw a
pencil line ⅜" (1cm) from and parallel to
one 9" (23cm) edge. Follow instructions
for pressing and stitching plain pleats on
page 34, forming pleats ¼" (5mm) wide
and ¾" (2cm) apart (fig 2).
2 Then topstitch each of the pleats with
3 lines of straight stitching, using a dark
needle thread and light bobbin thread
(see page 34).
3 Measure ½" (1.5cm) in from a side
edge, and again following instructions
for pressing and stitching plain pleats on
page 34, stitch 3 parallel lines, each 4"
(10cm) apart, in opposite directions, to
create a wave effect (fig 3).

To make the pillow cover

1 Trim pleated panel to measure 19"
(48cm) long. With right sides together,
stitch a plain front panel to each long
side of pleated panel just inside lines of
stitching that hold pleats in place.
2 Trim pleated square to same size as
back square. Leaving a ½" (12mm) seam
allowance, make the pillow cover,
incorporating the fringed edging and
inserting the zipper along one side.
Insert pillow form.

fig 3

Cream pleated pillow

Stitch methods

Set straight stitch
Tension: normal settings throughout
Feet: normal presser foot, zipper foot
Needle: 12/80

You will need

For a pillow 18" (45cm) square:
9" x 20½" (23 x 51cm) fine silk
19" x 38" (48 x 96cm) rough silk, plus
   20" x 38" (50 x 96cm) extra for bias
   strips
Matching sewing thread
3¼yd (3m) fine filler cord
14" (35cm) zipper
Pillow form to fit cover

To work the pleated panel

1 Press fine silk rectangle, and using a ruler and draftsman triangle, draw a pencil line ½" (1.5cm) from and parallel to one 9" (23cm) edge. Follow instructions for pressing and stitching plain pleats on page 34, forming pleats ⅜" (1cm) wide and ½" (1.5cm) apart, to make a panel 9" (23cm) square.
2 Measure ½" (1.5cm) in from a side edge, and again following instructions on page 34, stitch parallel lines each 2" (5cm) apart in opposite directions to create a wave effect.

To trim the pleated panel

1 Cut out 2 19" (48cm) squares from rough silk.
2 Cut extra fabric into bias strips 1½" (4cm) wide. Join to form a continuous strip 3¼yd (3m) long, and use to cover filler cord.
3 Pin a length of piping all around pleated square. Stitch close to cord, using a zipper foot. Trim seam allowances and fold underneath so that piping surrounds panel.

To make the pillow cover

1 Lay piped panel centrally on a rough silk square. Pin and slipstitch carefully in place, with stitches hidden under piping.
2 Stitch remaining piping around outside of pillow front, leaving a ½" (1.5cm) seam allowance.
3 Using other square of rough silk for pillow back, make pillow cover, leaving a ½" (1.5cm) seam allowance and inserting zipper along one side. Insert pillow form.

summer, winter bedspread

Quilting a bedspread by hand is a labor of love – quilting by machine is a much quicker and more feasible prospect. Our seasonal bedspread is made as two quilts that can be used singly on summer nights and buttoned together to form a warm winter cover. Either choose a bold printed design for the top side of the upper quilt to provide shapes to quilt around, or turn to pages 98–99 for some alternative quilting patterns. The under quilt is simply stitched with straight lines, forming a grid.

fig 1

fig 2

fig 3

Stitch methods

Set straight stitch
Tension: normal settings throughout
Feet: embroidery or quilting foot, normal presser foot
Needle: 14/90

You will need

For a finished bedspread 89" x 54" (226 x 135cm):
89" (226cm) bold floral fabric, 54" (135cm) wide
3 pieces calico, each 89" x 54" (226 x 135cm)
2 pieces medium-weight polyester batting, each 89" x 54" (226 x 135cm)
4 large spools sewing threads, in colors to match floral printing
1 large spool calico-colored sewing thread
1 large spool contrasting sewing thread, for under quilt
8½ yd (7.5m) double-fold bias binding, 1½ " (3.5cm) wide, for each quilt
4½ yd (3.9m) cotton tape, 1" (2.5cm) wide
26 buttons

Note: When quilting near the center of a quilt, roll up one side so that it fits easily under the sewing-machine arm.

To make the upper quilt

1 Following instructions on page 35 (Trapunto Quilting), make a quilting sandwich of floral fabric, batting, and calico. Pin and baste layers together.
2 Select flowers to be quilted, and mark them with a pin or tailor's tack.
3 Fit embroidery or quilting foot on machine, and thread bobbin with calico-colored thread. Quilt around flowers,

odd petals, stalks, and leaves, using needle-thread color appropriate for each outline.
4 Trim any uneven edges. Unfold one side of bias binding. Lay against floral fabric, right sides together and raw edges even. Pin or baste around the edges. Miter corners neatly (fig 1). Where binding ends meet, lay one inside the other and fold end of outer one to inside to form a neat join.
5 Using normal presser foot, stitch binding to quilt. Fold unstitched edge of binding to other side, and slipstitch to calico to cover the stitching line.
6 Spacing evenly, sew buttons around quilt edges on top side.

To make the under quilt

1 Following instructions on page 35, make a sandwich of calico, batting, and calico. Pin and baste layers together.
2 On calico, lightly mark an irregular grid of stitching lines from about 2¾" (7cm) to 6" (15cm) apart, using a sharp, hard pencil or vanishing pen. Fit embroidery or quilting foot on machine, and thread needle and bobbin with a color chosen from floral fabric (or use contrasting needle and bobbin threads). Stitch all lines in both directions, and trim any uneven edges.
3 Cut tape into 26 6" (15cm) lengths. Fold each strip in half, open out, and refold as shown in fig 2. Press all folds.
4 Lay under quilt over upper quilt, and mark all button positions.
5 Lay folded tapes at marked positions on side of quilt to lie against bed, with raw edges of tapes and quilt even (fig 3).
6 Bind quilt edges following steps 4 and 5 for upper quilt, then button quilts together to form a warm bedspread.

Free-motion stitching

Free-motion stitching in its most advanced form involves working without a machine foot and manually moving the fabric in any direction to form stitches. It can be viewed either as the really creative part of machine embroidery or absolutely terrifying! Like riding a bicycle, free-motion stitching is a technique which once learned is never forgotten; but as the wheels wobble underneath you, or the first faltering free-motion stitches are formed, it may seem unlikely that either skill is obtainable or even desirable. But try it; the skill needed can be acquired with a little practice and will open up a completely new range of stitching possibilities.

Beginning to free-motion stitch with a foot should be seen as a progression from machine darning. The first techniques described in this chapter are stitched with a darning foot with the machine feed disengaged. Once you have achieved free-motion stitching with a darning foot, try without; one method may feel more natural to you than the other.

free-motion embroidery with a foot

Learning to use a sewing machine for free-motion stitching is entirely a matter of practice. Confidence can be built up slowly – there is no need to choose a complex design as a first project, or to start free-motion stitching without using a foot. Most free-motion stitching designs can, in fact, be worked with or without the use of a foot, and there are advantages and disadvantages to each.

Some simple outlines and designs that are ideal for practicing free-motion stitching are given on pages 100–101. First experiments may have to be consigned to the wastebasket, but any interesting effects – whether planned or accidental – should be kept, along with a note of how they were achieved. Other successful attempts can be mounted together to form a sampler, or can be made into greetings cards.

Setting up the machine

DROP THE FEED DOGS!

There is very little difference in setting up the machine for set or free-motion stitching. Threading the machine is just the same; the only alteration necessary for free-motion stitching is adjusting the feed teeth to allow the fabric to be moved freely by hand. Certain embroidery effects will require alterations to the zigzag width or to the tension.

Feed teeth

In set stitching, the motion of the feed teeth (see page 11) moves the fabric under the needle. In free-motion stitching, the fabric is controlled by hand and may be moved in any direction, as well as forward and backward.
• First lower or cover the feed teeth. Most sewing machines, and particularly those with embroidery or darning facilities, will have retractable feed teeth.
• Some sewing machines with fixed feed teeth will have a cover that clips or screws over the needle plate.
• If your sewing machine has neither option, unscrew the needle plate, and see if it is possible to remove the feed teeth temporarily, replacing the needle plate for stitching.
• As a last resort, tape a small piece of cardboard or plastic that has a central hole for the needle to pass through over the needle plate.

Stitch length

Stitch length should be set to 0. The length of the stitches is determined by moving the fabric manually.

Zigzag width

Zigzag width should usually be set to 0, although altering it can create a variety of textural effects, from blocks of color to random patterns (see page 60).

Tension

Drop feed dog lever to bottom (or ½ way on some)

The tension may not need altering when moving from set to free-motion stitching. If the stitching is not satisfactory, try loosening the needle-thread tension slightly. Altering either the needle-thread or bobbin tension to create unusual effects is an often-used technique in machine embroidery (see pages 61 and 92–93).

Needle and bobbin threads

Choose the same type of thread for the needle and bobbin for early experiments with free-motion stitching – a stronger or heavier weight thread will cause a weaker one to break. (For successful methods of using uneven threads to obtain special effects, see page 93).

Whether to use the same color for the needle and bobbin threads is a matter of personal preference.
• Using the same color will give a more intense hue, especially when working on fine fabrics. *TOP TIGHT!*
• If the tension settings have not been perfectly adjusted, some bobbin thread may show on the right side of the piece. This can be developed into a shading technique (see page 61), but if it is not intentional, using matching colors will disguise the problem.
• Using a single bobbin color for a whole project is quicker.

Using a darning foot

Many sewing machines will come with a darning foot or can be fitted with a standard one; some will also have one or more free-motion embroidery feet (see page 12).

A darning foot is usually made from clear plastic and has a spring mechanism, so that it bounces over uneven fabrics or areas of stitching but holds the fabric in place for the needle to enter smoothly. A darning foot should always be used when working on fabrics without an embroidery hoop.

I hold my fingers quite close as my instructor, Rosemary Eichorn, does. the result is better control.

Advantages

• For the inexperienced, the darning foot may offer more protection to fingers.
• For free-flowing designs, it may help the stitching to move across the fabric more freely.
• It is easier to stitch very stiff or heavily worked areas with a darning foot.

Disadvantages

• Even though the foot may be clear, it does restrict visibility of the immediate stitching area, making accurate detail stitching difficult. *TRUE!*
• In textured or heavily worked areas, the darning foot may become caught under loops of thread.

Starting to stitch

Begin free-motion stitching using a darning foot so that the only difference in the machine is the absence of the feed teeth and the only new technique to learn is moving the fabric by hand.

1 For first attempts, back each piece of fabric with a sew-in interfacing (stitch the two layers together around the outer edges using set straight stitch), or experiment with tear-away stabilizers under the embroidery area (see page 15). Finer fabrics can always be stretched in a hoop when using a darning foot (see pages 50–51).

2 Hold the fabric flat against the machine bed, either by pressing your fingers on the needle plate on either side of the darning foot (fig 1), or by holding the outer edges of the fabric but keeping your thumbs down so that the fabric is flat (fig 2). Do not stretch the fabric, but insure that the stitching area is taut.

3 Hold the threads to the back to avoid knotting, and start to stitch. Secure the threads at the beginning by working a few stitches in the same hole or by working a few backstitches. Using a medium machine speed, move the fabric slowly – if you do not move the fabric manually it will remain stationary, and a knot will quickly form.

Concentrate on creating a line of stitches rather than one stitch at a time. Stitches can be any length, but begin by making them quite small (about a 3mm long stitch setting, or 8 stitches per inch). Tiny stitches are difficult to make evenly, and long ones tend to pull the needle and thread, causing either one or both to break.

4 The stitches can be made in any direction, including backward, sideways, and in circles. Before attempting to work a particular design, experiment with straight lines worked in different directions, loops, S shapes, circles, and repeating linear patterns (see pages 100–101). Practice stitching lines close together to create a block of color, or stitching an outline and filling it in.

5 After working, pull all the threads to the back of the work, knot, and trim.

Problem solving

• If the bobbin thread shows at each change of direction, loosen the needle-thread tension slightly.
• If the machine is skipping stitches, the fabric may be too loose. Hold it more tautly, stiffen it with a heavier weight of interfacing (see above), or stretch it in a hoop. Alternatively, the needle may be blunt or bent and should be changed.
• Move the fabric smoothly, since pulling or jerking might break the needle.

decorated box

Making separate stiffened panels is an ideal way to practice free-motion stitching. The stiffener creates a fabric firm enough to stitch without an embroidery hoop, and the technique used employs a darning foot to give confidence to the nervous embroiderer!

Each panel is a sandwich of outer fabric, valance stiffener, and lining fabric, held together with set straight stitch. Because some of the decorative stitching on the box is also part of the construction, the machine will need to be altered more than once from free-motion to set stitching and back to free-motion stitching.

Choose fabrics and threads from the same palette of colors so that each panel can be used as an individual sampler of stitch effects but, when joined together, they will form a delightful embroidered box.

Stitch methods

Set straight stitch
Set zigzag stitch
Free-motion straight stitch
Couching with string
Tension: normal settings throughout
Feet: normal presser foot, darning foot
Needle: 14/90

You will need

For a box about 5½" (14cm) high:
4" x 28" (10 x 71cm) blue crêpe de chine
4" x 16" (10 x 40cm) purple crêpe de chine
4" x 20" (10 x 50cm) gold iridescent silk
4" (10cm) squares dark blue crêpe de chine, violet iridescent silk, and red organza
4" (10cm) valance stiffener, 44" (110cm) wide
6" (15cm) square fusible web
Rayon machine embroidery thread:
  1 spool of burnt orange and charcoal
  2 spools indigo
  1 spool multicolor
1 spool gold metallic machine embroidery thread
25" (64cm) string dyed with blue ink
16" (40cm) undyed string
2 flat copper beads
8 small iridescent beads
Thin cardboard for templates

To prepare the panels

1 From cardboard, cut out a 3½" (9cm) square and a roof triangle, using template on page 49. Use these templates to cut out 5 squares and 4 triangles from valance stiffener. Trim ⅛" (3mm) off each side of one square.

2 Use templates to cut out fabric squares and triangles, each ⅛" (3mm) larger all around than templates. Cut out 5 squares and 4 triangles from blue crêpe de chine, 4 squares from purple crêpe de chine, and 1 square and 4 triangles from gold iridescent silk.

3 Pin valance stiffener shapes between 2 fabric layers to create a sandwich with fabric right side out on each side (fig 1). Enclose 4 large squares between blue and purple crêpe de chine, and a smaller square and 4 triangles between blue crêpe de chine and gold iridescent silk.

fig 1

fig 2

To work the blue side panels

1 Work 2 side panels with blue crêpe de chine upward. Using indigo needle and bobbin threads and a normal presser foot, straight stitch up and down each panel in parallel lines.

2 Cut out 2 1½" (4cm) squares in gold silk and 2 in red organza. Lay organza on gold silk, and pin centrally on each blue panel. Straight stitch in place ¼" (6mm) from raw edges. Set stitch length to 1mm and zigzag to 2.5mm. Stitch over straight-stitched line to form a solid satin-stitched square. Change top thread to multicolor, stitch length and zigzag to 3mm, and stitch over satin-stitched square (fig 2). Fray small square edges.

3 Using the photographs on the left as a guide, mark positions of 4 corner spirals, suns, and moons with a sharp pencil. Draw a bird in 1 center square and a tree in the other, using templates opposite. Change to darning foot, and retract or cover feed. Set to straight stitch, and stitch spirals, using multicolor thread. Change needle thread to gold, and stitch suns and moons. Change needle thread to indigo, and stitch bird and tree motifs.

4 Trim panel edges. Change to normal presser foot, and lift or uncover feed. Change top thread to charcoal, set stitch length to 1mm and zigzag to 3.5mm, and satin stitch around edge of each panel. Change top thread to multicolor, stitch length to 3mm and zigzag to 4mm, and oversew around each panel.

5 Hand sew an iridescent bead to each corner of the central squares.

To work the purple side panels

1 Using normal presser foot and indigo needle thread, straight stitch around outside of each square, with purple side up. Cut out 2 1½" (4cm) squares of blue crêpe de chine and 2 1¼" (3.5cm) squares of violet iridescent silk, and back each small square with fusible web. Lay small squares centrally over larger squares, and larger squares centrally on purple side panels, and fuse in position.

2 Use photograph below left as a guide to stitch positions. Change needle thread to gold, and straight stitch a line on each side of central squares, using a triple stitch facility (see page 23) or, with stitch length at 3mm, stitching forward and back to form a thick line. Straight stitch twice around each central square.

3 Cut 4 4" (10cm) lengths of dyed string. Change needle thread to multicolor, set stitch length and zigzag to 3mm, lay lengths of string across top and bottom of each panel, and zigzag stitch over them. This technique is called "couching" (see page 72).

4 Change to darning foot, and retract or cover feed teeth. Set to straight stitch and stitch random spirals and scrolls around each central square. Change needle thread to indigo, and outline a diamond on each central square.

5 Using gold thread, hand sew a flat copper bead in center of each square, creating a cross with stitching.

6 Finish outer edge of each panel, following instructions in step 4 for blue side panels.

To work the roof

1 Stitch all roof panels gold side up, with longest edge of each triangle as base. Using normal presser foot and indigo needle thread, straight stitch parallel lines up and down 2 panels. Change to multicolor needle thread. Straight stitch parallel lines on second pair of panels.

2 Change needle thread to gold, stitch length to 1.5mm, and zigzag to 3mm, and using photograph on left as a placement guide, couch circles of dyed string onto 2 panels. Change needle thread to indigo, and using varied stitch length settings, couch spirals of undyed string on second pair of panels.

3 Using template below as a guide, draw a narrow 5-pointed star in the center of each couched circle with a sharp pencil. Change to darning foot, and retract or cover feed teeth. Change needle thread to gold, and set to straight stitch. Stitch the outline of each star, then fill it in with a block of indigo stitching.

4 Trim rough edges of panels. Change to normal presser foot, and lift or uncover feed teeth. Set stitch length to 1mm and zigzag to 3.5mm, and satin stitch around edge of panels, using indigo needle thread on panels with spirals and burnt orange on panels with stars.

To assemble the box

1 With gold side of base square up, straight stitch parallel lines up and down square, using indigo needle thread. Trim and finish raw edges with satin stitch as for step 4 of blue side panels.

2 Change needle and bobbin threads to burnt orange. Lay a blue side panel on a purple one with right sides together. Set stitch length and zigzag to 4mm, and join two side edges together. Repeat until all 4 sides are joined, making sure all sides are right way up.

3 Overcast stitch bottom of box to sides neatly by hand.

4 Machine stitch roof panels together, using charcoal needle thread and burnt orange bobbin thread. Place star panels on top so that charcoal thread is over burnt-orange edges and vice versa. Stitch over bottom edges of panels so that colors contrast. Leave a small hole in center of roof.

5 Make a tassel by wrapping a length of each thread color around 4 fingers, 5 times. Use a needle and thread to secure loop, bind threads together, secure with a stitch, and run needle back to secured end (fig 3). Push secured end into center of roof, and catch in place with a few stitches. Trim ends of tassel.

roof triangle

fig 3

49

free-motion embroidery without a foot

Free-motion machine embroidery worked without a foot, extends the techniques acquired for free-motion stitching with a darning foot. The methods used overcome some of the difficulties encountered when using a darning foot. The main advantage to stitching without a foot is that it allows a clear view of the stitching area. Also, an embroidery hoop is almost invariably used, holding the fabric flat and restricting the hand position to holding the frame so that there is little danger of stitching through a finger.

Most designs can be worked with or without a darning foot, so it really is a matter of personal preference, but try stitching without a foot, because it may suddenly reveal all kinds of new possibilities in your work. A selection of designs on which to practice is given on pages 100–101. ← PRACTICE DESIGNS!

Using a hoop

It is essential to stretch the fabric tightly and evenly for machine embroidering, and the easiest way of doing this is to use an embroidery hoop. Wooden hoops are the most suitable since they grip the fabric very tightly, although other types can improved by binding (see page 16).

fig 1

fig 2

• Fix the fabric in the reverse manner to that used for hand embroidery, with the working surface (right side) at the bottom of the frame, so the underside will lie flat against the machine bed for stitching (see page 16).
• Choose a comfortable position for holding the hoop. This depends to a degree on its size, but since the movement of the hoop controls the stitching, it is important to find the position that insures maximum control. Try one of the two methods shown in figs 1 and 2, and do not grip the hoop too tightly – an absorbing design may require long periods of stitching, and clenched fingers will create tension in your hands, arms, and shoulders.
• For some projects a hoop size has been given, but it is a guide rather than a command: use the size of hoop that is most comfortable to hold. For small areas, it is advisable to have the entire design within the ring, but for larger pieces, it is much easier to use a smaller hoop and move the fabric as necessary than to try to maneuver a wheel!
• Before transferring a design onto fabric, insure that there is a sufficient fabric allowance around the design to fix it into the hoop. Position the area to be worked in the center of the hoop.

Setting up the machine

Set up the machine as for free-motion stitching with a darning foot (see pages 44–45), omitting the foot. Setting up the machine, lowering or covering the feed teeth, and setting the stitch length and tension soon becomes automatic, but until it does, always run through the sequence of changing the machine from set to free-motion stitching. When using an unfamiliar machine or one which has been unused for a while, work a few lines of set straight stitch on scrap fabric to insure that the machine is running smoothly and correctly, then change to the free-motion stitching settings.

Starting to stitch

The technique for free-motion embroidery is just the same with or without a foot: the stitch length is set to 0 and the feed teeth are lowered, so it is the hoop movement that will determine the stitch length and direction.

1 It is vital to lower the presser bar before starting to stitch, otherwise the needle tension will not be engaged. The loose threads are more likely to tangle, so bring both to the top of the fabric and hold them behind the needle.

2 Secure the needle and bobbin threads by either stitching on the spot a few times or backstitching.

3 Become accustomed to working at medium speed, since working slowly actually increases control problems. Concentrate on moving the hoop, first stitching straight lines in different directions and then building up confidence with curves and circles.

4 Secure the threads at the end. When changing the needle color only, leave the bobbin thread uncut but stitch on the spot to secure the new color.

Technical stitching problems, such as needle and thread breakages, are more likely with free-motion embroidery. If the machine is running well for set stitching, it is probably your technique that is at fault, so refer to Problem Solving, below.

Embroidery techniques

The techniques detailed here are equally suitable for working with or without a darning foot. Try both methods, following the general instructions for both to determine which feels most comfortable.

• Start with combinations of straight lines. Work parallel lines by moving the hoop up and down or from side to side. Make the lines closer and closer together, until they form a solid block.

• Move the hoop in small curves and circles, creating loops and wiggles. Vermicelli stitch (top left), which is worked as a series of semi-circles stitched in alternate directions, creates an interesting texture. Lots of tiny circles worked close together and overlapping each other create a filling stitch called seed stitch (center left).

• Practice methods of outlining shapes. Work freehand or over a pencilled line, and compare the effect of one line of outline stitching with two or more.

• Work blocks of solid color within the outlines. Practice creating a dense area of stitching with no fabric showing.

• Work several blocks of color, at first stitching up to the outline and then over it, so that the areas of color meet neatly with no outline showing.

• Blocks of stitching can be worked in different directions, creating interesting shading as the light reflects off the threads in different ways. However, stitching blocks at different angles tends to distort the fabric, so if the finished embroidery needs to be flat and cannot be stretched or mounted, it is safer to work all the blocks with parallel lines of machine stitching.

• Experiment with using different colors together and with enhancing a palette of color by introducing a complete contrast, such as black (bottom left).

Problem solving

• If the needle thread breaks, it may be being held too tightly as stitching starts, or the needle-thread tension may need to be loosened slightly. Alternatively, the thread may be looping into the bobbin case and breaking. Check the underside for loops, then tighten the needle-thread tension if necessary.

• If the bobbin thread does not hold, check to see if it has broken. If not, the fabric may be too loose in the hoop. Natural fabrics are easier to stitch than synthetics, but using a ballpoint or thicker needle often solves the problem.

• Machine embroidery threads are not as tough as sewing threads and may break when being forced into heavily worked areas or tough fabrics. Using a larger needle may help.

• Blunt needles will skip stitches, so change them before they bend or break. As a guide, the Book Cover on pages 56–59 would need at least three replacement needles.

If the needle breaks continually, either it is being pulled by attempting to make stitches that are too big, or the needle has been inserted in the machine back to front or not high enough.

silk lampshade

A machine-embroidered design need not be complicated or time-consuming to work. Sometimes a very simple application can be equally – or even more – effective than a heavily worked one. Here, softly layered drapes of silk and organza are caught together with small spots of vermicelli stitching. The choice of colors is all-important, so spend time laying different tones of organza over the underlayer of slubbed silk. This shade is a combination of three spicy colors from the same palette, but contrasts – such as blue over red to create purple, or two similar fabric colors highlighted with contrasting spots of embroidery – could be just as effective. Before stitching, the organza is cut away at the points to be embroidered to reveal the true color of the silk below.

Stitch method

Set straight stitch
Set zigzag stitch
Free-motion straight stitch
Tension: normal settings throughout
Foot: normal presser foot for finishing lampshade
Needles: 12/80

You will need

To cover a lampshade 10" (25.5cm) in diameter and 6" (15cm) deep:
White or cream lampshade
32" x 39" (80 x 100cm) slubbed silk
36" (90cm) square organza
1 spool toning rayon machine embroidery thread
Sewing threads to match silk and organza
Tape or ribbon
Small embroidery hoop
Fabric glue

To cut out

1 Fabrics to cover lampshade are cut as complete circles. Measure 2 sides and across top of lampshade (A, A, and B in fig 1) and add together. Add another 6" (15cm) for extra fullness and hems: total is diameter of silk circle.
2 Place one end of a length of tape in center of silk, and pin. Measure half diameter length along tape from pin, and mark. Hold central pin and rotate taut tape, drawing a circle on silk with a soft pencil held at marked point on tape (fig 2). In center of circle, mark a circle 1¼" (3cm) less in diameter than measurement B on fig 1. Cut out around both circles.
3 Add 2" (5cm) to larger circle diameter, then halve this measurement, and mark a circle on organza as above (if pencil will not work on organza, mark with pins). Mark a central circle to same size as for silk. Cut out around both circles.

fig 1

fig 2

To work the embroidery

1 Fold silk circle in half, in half again, and in half once more. Finger-press along folds so that when circle is unfolded 8 creases at even intervals are obvious.

2 Lay organza circle over silk with an even overlap all around, and pin together along creases with 3 evenly spaced pins on each. On alternate creases, first pin should be about ¾" (2cm) further away from circle center (fig 3). These pins mark positions of embroidered dots, so lay fabric circles over lampshade to check that the dots fall within desired lampshade area.

3 At each pinned position, cut a ½" (12mm) diameter hole *in organza only*.

4 Set sewing machine for free-motion embroidery, with feed teeth covered or lowered, no foot, tension normal, and stitch length and zigzag set to 0. Thread needle and bobbin with toning embroidery thread. Place fabrics in hoop with a hole in center, and stitch over hole with vermicelli stitch (page 51). Stitching should extend beyond raw edge of hole and hold fabrics together.

To finish lampshade

1 Set sewing machine for set stitching, with feed teeth up, normal presser foot, tension normal, and stitch length set to 3mm. Change needle and bobbin threads to sewing thread to match silk.

2 Measure circumference of silk circle, and cut out enough bias strips 1¼" (3cm) wide from remainder of silk to make a hem facing 3" (8cm) longer than circle circumference. With right sides together, join short ends of strips (fig 4), then press and trim seam allowances. With right sides together and raw edges even, lay bias strip around edge of silk circle. Pin, overlapping ends and folding short raw edge of underneath end to wrong side, then stitch around circle with a ⅝" (1.5cm) seam allowance.

3 Trim seam allowance. Then fold under and press a narrow turning along unstitched edge of facing, and press facing to wrong side of silk. Hand sew folded edge to silk with invisible slipstitches.

4 Finish organza edge by setting zigzag to 3mm, using sewing thread to match

fig 3

fig 4

fig 5

organza, and stitching just inside outer edge on right side – this stitching will automatically roll organza. Trim away excess fabric.

5 Lay circles centrally over lampshade, and make a series of cuts from central hole to just short of inside edge of shade (fig 5). Remove from shade. Fold organza and silk together to wrong side of silk, and pin. Lay over central hole to check that folded edge will fold neatly to inside

of hole; it may be necessary to lengthen some cuts. Catch raw edges to inside with hand stitches.

6 Apply a circle of fabric glue sparingly around top inside edge of lampshade, and following manufacturer's instructions, lightly press inner circle of fabrics onto glue. Apply tiny spots of glue to lampshade to hold silk to it in even folds; glue spots should fall under lines of stitched dots.

book cover

A large piece such as this notebook cover or a cover for a similar-sized book may appear daunting by virtue of its size, but once you have practiced a free-motion filling-stitch technique and feel confident creating a block of color, it is simply a matter of "coloring in". Filling the various areas of color and building up the design will then become a rhythmic and absorbing process. Work all the colored areas first and add the black blocks afterward, to create a strong contrast that will give definition to the design.

The method of stitching described is totally free-motion, without any foot, which allows a clear view of the stitching and build-up of color, but if you find footless stitching frightening, use a darning foot. As the finished embroidery will not be stretched or mounted, it is important to choose a firm fabric and to stitch all the colored blocks with the stitching lines following the grain of the fabric to prevent distortion.

Stitch methods
Set straight stitch
Free-motion straight stitch
Tension: normal settings throughout
Foot: normal presser foot for assembling
Needle: 14/90

You will need
To cover a 9" x 7" (23 x 17.5cm)
notebook cover:
1yd (80cm) medium-weight calico, 36"
    (90cm) wide
8" x 18" (20 x 45cm) thin batting
Cotton sewing thread in 109yd (100m)
    spools:
    4 spools lime green
    3 spools each pale green, jasmine
    yellow, flame, and gold
Cotton machine embroidery thread in
    219yd (200m) spools:
    2 spools each black and bright yellow
Cream sewing thread
7" (17cm) embroidery hoop
Fabric glue

Placement plan

To work the embroidery

1 Enlarge pattern outline, which shows cover front and half of spine, on page 59 to 110%, using a photocopier. Check that outer line of design is at least ¼" (6mm) larger than notebook cover to allow for contraction. For cover back, trace design. Reverse tracing, and tape it to left-hand side of spine (see placement plan on left).

2 Cut calico into 2 13¾" x 24¾" (35 x 63cm) rectangles. With marked grain line on straight grain of fabric, lay one rectangle centrally over pattern, with a wide margin of calico all around, and trace design.

3 Place top right-hand corner of design in embroidery hoop. Set sewing machine for free-motion stitching, with feed teeth lowered or covered, no foot, and stitch length and zigzag set to 0. Thread needle and bobbin with matching threads, and work each colored section by first outlining shape, then filling by stitching up and down parallel to shorter edges of calico. Remember always to lower foot lever before stitching, even though there is no foot (see page 50).

4 Fill in black sections after surrounding colored shapes have been embroidered. Because black sections are mostly smaller and finer, fill with stitches in whichever direction is most appropriate.

5 Embroider any border areas within hoop with stitches parallel to edges of book cover.

6 Move hoop along and repeat steps 3–5 until front of cover is complete. Then stitch back of cover, and finally spine.

7 Lay finished embroidery over design pattern. It will have contracted: bring back to its original size by increasing border widths.

8 Press embroidery, first on wrong and then on right side, using a steam iron on cotton setting.

To assemble the cover

1 Cut 2 rectangles of batting to fit patterned sections (without borders), and use a minimal dab of fabric glue in center of each patterned section to secure batting in place.

2 With right sides together and edges even, lay embroidered rectangle on second calico rectangle. Trim long top and bottom edges, leaving ⅝" (1.5cm) seam allowances. On each short edge, measure 3¾" (9.5cm) beyond embroidery, mark, and trim.

3 Set sewing machine for set stitching, with feed teeth up, normal presser foot, tension normal, and stitch length set to 3mm. Using cream sewing thread, stitch together side seams ⅝" (1.5cm) in from raw edges (fig 1). With calico fabric pieces lying perfectly flat, measure exactly 3¼" (8cm) in from each stitching line and make a mark.

4 Then create a pleat at one end of embroidery as shown in fig 2.

5 With wrong side of embroidery up, stitch along one long side on very edge of embroidery. Repeat along second side, leaving an 7" (18cm) gap for turning (fig 3).

6 Turn through, press, and overcast stitch gap by hand.

fig 1   fig 2   fig 3

Enlarge to 110% on a photocopier.

■ black □ jasmine yellow ■ bright yellow ■ gold ■ flame □ pale green ■ lime green

free-motion satin stitch

Using the stitch-width, or zigzag, control to alter the width of the stitch, while continuing to control the length manually (by moving the fabric or hoop), gives rise to a whole new range of embroidery techniques. While initial attempts to alter the width settings and control the size and direction of stitching may leave you longing for another pair of hands – persevere – there is a wealth of exciting effects that can be created by using the satin-stitch setting range.

Starting to stitch

Always use an embroidery hoop for free-motion zigzag and satin stitching, firstly because the fabric is far more likely to twist and pucker with the effect of the swing needle, and secondly because the fabric may have to be moved with one hand only, and making controlled movements single-handed without a hoop is impossible.

1 Start (and end) each line of zigzag or satin stitch by working a few straight stitches in one spot.
2 To begin with, set the stitch width and practice controlling the stitch length – uneven stitching will be much more obvious when using swing-needle settings. You will need to be able to create an even zigzag effect before attempting satin stitch, which is formed by moving the hoop so slowly that the stitches lie side by side.
3 Work a series of exaggerated loops, and then circles. Note that although the hoop can be moved in any direction, the swing needle only works from side to side, so the effect of the zigzag stitching is much more obvious when the hoop is being moved forward and backward than when it is being moved sideways.
4 Begin to alter the width settings, first working blocks of different widths and then altering the dial with your right hand as the hoop is being moved with your left, to create a graduated widening and narrowing.

For maximum control of the hoop, hold it with your left hand at the back (behind the needle) and your left arm resting on the machine bed.

Embroidery techniques

The Button Collection on pages 62–63 simply uses a zigzag setting to increase the dimpled effect of the filling stitch, but swing-needle settings can be used to create a great variety of effects, from an abstract pattern covering the fabric to small overstitched areas adding texture to straight-stitched embroidery. A range of outlines on which to practice is given on pages 102–103.

• Practice working straight lines both forward and backward, then experiment with creating wavy lines, working rows of lines side by side.
• Try working rows of satin stitch and then oversewing between them, with a narrow width setting.
• Work satin-stitch beads by securing threads with straight stitching on the spot, then setting the desired width and again stitching on the spot until a raised bead is created. Secure the thread, move to the next bead point, and repeat.
• Any automatic pattern settings on a sewing machine can be stitched in a free-motion manner and used to create further decorative effects.

Problem solving
• The needle thread may pull the bobbin thread to the surface (see opposite). If the effect is not desirable, loosen the needle-thread tension slightly. The looser stitching style may suit the embroidery.
• Turning neat corners while stitching may prove difficult. If so, stop stitching when the needle is inserted through the fabric on the outside point of the corner, and pivot the hoop around the needle before starting to stitch again.

tension techniques

With set stitching it is usually desirable to have an even needle-thread and bobbin tension Anyone who has ever attended needlework classes knows that to alter the tension settings on a sewing machine is to court disaster! Contrary to belief, however, altering the tension settings will not adversely affect the smooth running of the machine afterward – they can simply be reset. For machine embroiderers, using unusual tension techniques is a fascinating way of adding shades of color and texture to their work.

Simple tension changes

For guidance on achieving perfect tension and on how to alter both needle-thread and bobbin tension, see page 11. There are some embroidery techniques for which it is desirable to have a tight bobbin tension that will pull the top threads to the underside of the work and these are described in detail on pages 92–93, but for the more gentle textural effects created in this chapter, the bobbin thread is drawn up to appear on the top of the work, and this can be achieved by tightening the needle-thread tension.

Starting to stitch

Always start by stitching a test row with normal tensions to use as a control, and remember to look at the underside of the stitching as well as the top surface to see what effects the altered tension settings are creating.

1 Mount the fabric in an embroidery hoop – this is essential.
2 For practice stitching, thread the needle and bobbin with the same thread but in contrasting colors. This will make it much easier to judge the effects as each tension is altered.
3 If only a small alteration is required, it is quicker and easier to alter the needle-thread tension only, but tightening one tension and not compensating by loosening the other may cause the unaltered thread to snap more often, especially as the tension is increased. If the thread begins to snap, loosen the bobbin tension to compensate for the tightened needle-thread tension.
4 Hold the threads toward the back of the machine when starting to stitch, otherwise the bobbin thread will not be under tension and may well loop up on the back of the work.
5 When you have finished embroidering, readjust the tension settings to normal.

Embroidery techniques

The tension techniques described here are intended to be subtle. They are used to create shading of color and texture on the Button Collection on pages 62–63, and could be used for a similar effect in the grass area of the picture on pages 66–69.

• The filling stitch on the buttons has a tightened needle-thread tension which, when used with contrasting threads at needle and bobbin, creates a speckled texture. Choosing a zigzag setting of 1mm or 2mm will create a more random stitching effect.
• Use a fast stitch speed, and move the hoop slowly to create a filling stitch suitable for the buttons or picture.
• Reversing the needle and bobbin colors creates a subtle change. Using matching thread gives a more intense color.

Problem solving
• Stitching on the spot can create decorative bobbles but will increase the likelihood of the thread snapping, so try to keep an even pace of stitching.
• If the bobbin tension is too tight it will pull the needle thread down into loops, which may well catch in the shuttle race.
• For free satin stitch with a tightened needle-thread tension, loosening the bobbin tension creates a softer effect, whereas tightening the top tension only can create a rather, taut top line.

61

button collection

Like the box panels on pages 46–49, button covers are an ideal project on which to practice new techniques or experiment with different designs. They can be worked on small scraps from your workbasket, or on a lightweight calico or similar fabric. Choose a limited range of colors – seven or eight is ideal – and work each button using a selection of three colors from the palette, plus a metallic thread to add a rich, jewel-like quality.

Use the individual designs to experiment with the needle-thread tension; use one color in the needle and another in the bobbin; try different tensions; then reverse the needle and bobbin colors – all this will build up your knowledge of the multitude of shades and textures that can be created using a limited range of colors. The completed buttons will form a complementary set of individual designs and can be used to enliven a dull pillow or dress up a plain jacket. Alternative designs can be found on pages 108–109.

Stitch methods
Free-motion straight stitch
Free-motion satin stitch
Tension: normal or needle-thread only tightened
Foot: darning foot
Needle: 12/80 or 10/70

You will need
Light calico or similar fabric scraps
Sheer fabric scraps (organza is ideal)
Assorted machine embroidery threads
Gold metallic machine embroidery thread
Embroidery hoop
Easy-cover button molds
Thin cardboard for templates

FABRIC SIZES

To prepare the fabric
1 For each size of easy-cover button mold, 3 circular cardboard templates are needed: 1 with diameter equal to that of button mold (area of main design); 1 with diameter ¼" (6mm) larger (allows design to continue and cover sides); 1 with diameter 1½" (2mm) larger (extra to be clipped into back of button mold to hold fabric in place). Using a compass and pencil, draw and cut out 3 appropriate cardboard circles.
2 For each button, use templates to draw 3 concentric circles on calico. Draw one of the heart designs above left onto the central circle, choose a design from pages 108–109, or make your own.

3 Set sewing machine for free-motion stitching with a darning foot and feed teeth lowered or covered. Set stitch length and zigzag to 0. Thread needle and bobbin with thread to match the chosen color of organza.
4 Fix calico in hoop. Cut organza piece slightly larger than largest circle, and lay over it. Stitch around the 2 larger circles to hold organza in place.

To work the embroidery
1 Change either needle or bobbin thread to a contrasting color, tighten needle-thread tension, set zigzag to 1mm or 2mm if desired, and fill in all areas of one color. Change one of the thread colors, and fill in next area of color.
2 Continue changing colors and filling in until design is complete. On some buttons, areas of organza can be left unstitched or a motif can be added over base stitching.
3 Thread needle and bobbin with gold thread, loosen needle-thread tension again. With zigzag set to 0, separate areas of color with lines of straight stitch. Motifs can be highlighted with 2 or more lines of straight stitching.

To finish buttons
Cut out around outer calico circle. Following manufacturer's instructions, catch fabric onto serrated under-edge of button front. Clip on back (fig 1).

fig 1

63

picture techniques

Embroidering a picture is only frightening because it changes the project from a practical one requiring certain machine-sewing skills into an artistic achievement. If you find the idea of stitching a picture more challenging than stitching a pattern, think of the picture simply as outlines to fill in, and adding the fine details merely as additional features or decorations. The style of the finished picture is entirely personal, but to begin with, simple naïve drawings are the easiest to translate into an embroidered work, since they use blocks of color and strong outlines.

Stitching a picture

The stitching used for a picture can include some or all of the techniques described earlier in this chapter. The fabric should be held in an embroidery hoop and the machine set up for free-motion stitching, with or without a darning foot.

Whether to use only straight stitch and a normal tension setting, or to introduce some satin stitching and tightened needle-thread tension, is a personal choice. It is tempting to use the same bobbin thread throughout, but changing it to match the needle thread will create more intense colors.

1 For a small picture, center the design in the hoop; for a larger picture, which will need to be moved within the hoop as areas are completed, begin stitching near the center, and move outward to avoid distorting the fabric too much.
2 Work the outlines first, using black or dark gray thread. There is no need to cut the threads between outlines as they are stitched. When the outlines have been completed, trim away loose threads on the right side and leave on the reverse.
3 Work each block of color just up to its dark outline – if some outlines are visible on the final picture, they will simply look like sketch lines. Practice joining blocks of color neatly: it is a mistake to stitch around each outlined area with the self color, because this will create separate blocks. These could be effective on the Book Cover (see pages 56–59), but would detract from a picture.
4 Within each area of color, concentrate on working parallel lines of stitches to create a neat coloring technique, but alter the direction of stitching of different areas to suit the design. For instance, where the girl's legs bend (above left), curve the lines of stitching to follow the leg contours.

Techniques for larger areas

You can work the areas of background around objects in the picture as they are completed, which will leave you with less monotonous stitching to do at the end but does not allow for any late changes to the design. You can leave all the background until the rest of the picture is complete, then decide whether the plain background needs to be a slightly different color than that originally planned, or if the use of a tightened needle-thread tension would add some desirable texture.

Tightening the needle-thread tension (see page 61) and using the same color in the needle and bobbin would add a slight texture to a single-colored area. Using a contrasting bobbin color with the tension technique could create a range of other effects. For example, try a silver bobbin thread with dark blue for a starry sky, or green with a yellow bobbin thread for a field of buttercups.

If filling in large areas of color is daunting, cheat! You can work the embroidery on a suitable colored fabric, appliqué pieces of colored fabric in place, or use fabric paints to color the background areas.

[handwritten note at bottom:] Tightening the needle tension brings UP the bobbin thread in small dots to larger dots. It's nice, mottled color. If the top thread matches the fabric – the bobbin dot colors are like pointillism – nice shading technique

Working fine details

important!

There are two methods of working details such as facial features. You can either work them first and fill in the stitching around them, or wait until all the other stitching is done and then work the details.

(1) If the details are worked first, there is a much better chance of unpicking them successfully if they do go wrong – unpicking and removing small stitches that are worked into a mass of other stitches is practically impossible to achieve. However, there is a danger that the finer details will disappear under the surrounding stitches. Details worked (2) on top of the background stitches will be slightly raised and therefore look more prominent.

Whichever method is used, it is safest to pull both the threads at the start and finish off each piece of stitching to the reverse, then tie them together to insure that they are secured.

Finishing edges

There are two methods of finishing picture edges. The first method can be used for pictures with straight edges, while the second is more suitable for pictures with uneven edges, which machine embroidered pieces often have.

fig 1

fig 2

• For the first method, fuse double-sided hemming tape along the four edges of the embroidery, on the reverse side of the picture. Trim the fabric to the width of the hemming tape, and fold it over so that the picture edge is just rolled to the back. Carefully trim away excess fabric at the corners, and press to adhere (fig 1).

• For the second finishing method, baste strips of tear-away fabric stabilizer or vanishing muslin (see page 80) over the four edges on the reverse side of the picture (fig 2). Turn the picture over so right side is up.

• Then for both methods, set the sewing machine for set satin stitch, with feed teeth up, normal presser foot and tension, stitch length set at 1mm and zigzag at 4mm. Stitch all around the outer edge of the picture: if the outer edges are folded under, the outside stitch of the satin stitch should be worked over the folded edge. If the edges are unfolded (the second method), the inside stitch of the satin stitch should be worked over the edge of the picture stitching all the way around. Then tear away the stabilizer or vanishing muslin, and trim the fabric to the satin stitch.

Problem solving

• Rest the machine every 20 minutes to insure that it does not overheat.

• Change the needles before they bend, break, or become blunt – blunt needles will skip stitches.

• If the work has become distorted during the stitching process, press it under a barely damp cloth. Do not press heavily, as the weight will flatten the embroidered stitches.

• If the work is very distorted, dampen and stretch it (see page 19), then leave to dry completely before lacing it over a piece of cardboard.

lying on a rug

Embroidering a figurative picture might seem an impossible achievement, but the embroidery techniques are actually no different than those used for the Book Cover or Button Collection projects earlier in this chapter. The secret of success is to start small and to practice. Enlarge and trace the cat, two or three potted plants, or the head from the design on page 69. Draw a square or rectangle around the outline, and stitch onto calico stretched in an embroidery hoop. The practice pieces can be mounted and used as greetings cards. Skills at filling areas of color and working fine details will be quickly acquired. Continue to work small, simple pictures, drawing inspiration from postcards, pictures, or photographs, and you will gradually build up the skills and confidence to embroider a large picture.

Stitch methods

Free-motion straight stitch
Set straight stitch
Tension: normal or needle-thread only tightened
Foot: darning foot, normal presser foot
Needle: 12/80

You will need

For a finished picture 8" x 10¼"
(20 x 26cm):
16" x 20" (40 x 50cm) heavyweight calico
1 spool each rayon machine embroidery thread in colors shown on chart, plus 1 extra spool background green
1 spool multicolor rayon machine embroidery thread, for stripes on cat
1 spool silver metallic machine embroidery thread, for cat's whiskers
5 skeins cotton embroidery floss in colors to coordinate with picture
Black sewing thread
15¼" x 18" (38.5 x 45cm) cardboard for mounting
8" (20cm) wooden embroidery hoop
Fusible hemming web or tear-away fabric stabilizer

To work the embroidery

1 Enlarge picture patterns on the right to 110%, using a photocopier. Then transfer the picture centrally onto the calico, using a sharp pencil. Stretch calico into embroidery hoop.

2 Set sewing machine for free-motion stitching with a darning foot, feed teeth lowered or covered, tension normal, and black thread at top and bobbin. Work all the outlines first.

3 Following key and diagram opposite, fill in blocks of color, always using same color thread in needle and bobbin. Alter needle-thread tension if desired for some areas (see page 61).

4 Move hoop, and continue to fill areas of color until picture is complete.

5 Finish picture edges, using one of the methods described on page 65.

6 Hold long lengths of floss together. Starting a little way in from one corner of picture, hold lengths against picture edge, and lightly twist them together to form a cord. Set sewing machine for set stitching, with stitch length and zigzag set at 4mm, and zigzag over cord, attaching it to picture with outside stitch of zigzag (fig 1). Fold cord crisply around corners. Overlap cord ends neatly so that cut edges all lie under picture on reverse side (fig 2).

To mount the picture

1 Lay picture centrally on a piece of cardboard. With pencil point under twisted cord (so line will be hidden), draw around edge of picture.

2 With a sewing needle, pierce holes at ½" (1.5m) intervals. Using black sewing thread, lace picture to cardboard with tiny stitches into reverse edge of picture and long stitches under cardboard.

fig 1

fig 2

Enlarge to 110% on a photocopier.

■ black *cat, girl's and ginger cat's features*

■ bright pink *girl's cheeks, rug border, and trowel handle*

□ pale pink *skin tone*

■ dark brown *hair*

■ warm brown *earth*

■ terracotta *flowerpots*

□ blue-gray *trowel*

■ pale gray *black cat's features*

■ ocher *ginger cat, spots on earth*

■ violet *dress*

■ blue *stripes on rug*

■ emerald *spots on rug*

■ bright green *grass*

■ jade *plants*

■ dark green *lines on grass and edging*

■ gold *rug*

■ multicolor *stripes on ginger cat*

□ silver *whiskers*

69

Decorative effects

Learning to free-motion stitch opens up a wonderful variety of effects with which lines or blocks of color can be created. This final chapter explores the additional possibilities for unusual stitch effects that are offered by altering the stitch tension settings, or by stitching on vanishing fabric.

In perfect set stitching, the needle and bobbin threads twist within the fabric so that no needle thread appears below and no bobbin thread on top. Altering the tension settings allows one thread to pull the other through the fabric, forming raised lines or exaggerated loops far removed from the sedate progression of set stitches.

Vanishing fabrics provide a temporary surface on which to stitch. This surface is then removed, leaving the stitches to form a new fabric. All kinds of designs can be worked using this technique, from precise grids to insubstantial lacy wisps or rich embroidered tapestries, which, although hard to believe, can be stitched by an ordinary sewing machine!

letters & monograms

Mention machine embroidery, and monograms on towels or bathrobes immediately spring to mind. In fact, the very wide, graduated lines of a traditional satin-stitch monogram can only be created with an industrial machine or a computerized domestic model. However, although it is impossible to reproduce those flat satin-stitch letters, decorative lettering may be stitched in a variety of other ways using any swing-needle sewing machine, and the handwritten quality of the letters creates a particularly charming effect.

Choosing letters

On pages 104–105 there is a choice of alphabets, including one of capitals that could be used for initials, and a flowing, lower-case script that would be ideal for embroidering a message on a drawstring bag, adding simple detail in self-colored thread on bed or table linen, or working an apt quote on a pillow or chair back. Alternatively, use either your own handwriting or that of the person to whom you will be giving the finished piece, and enlarge it on a photocopier to an appropriate size. As a guide, the small letters on the Pieced Tablecloth on pages 74–79 are ¾" (2cm) high.

Stitching techniques

The lettering styles shown on these two pages are much more free-flowing and personal than an industrially stitched monogram, but it is still important that each letter should be distinct – a single line of straight stitch, for example, would fade into insignificance on all but the smallest project. The first method given here is couching, which uses set machine stitching. The other methods employ free-motion stitching.

Set-stitched couching

fig 1

Set-stitched letters with couching

Set-stitched letters tend to be very angular. One of the simplest ways of creating a more flowing script is to sew a length of fine cord over the lines of the letters, using set stitching with a zigzag width slightly wider than the cord. Sew over but not through the cord so that it is caught, or "couched," in place.

- Some machines have a cording foot, which holds the cord in the correct position while stitching; if your machine does not have this facility, wrap an adhesive tape around an open-toe presser foot, set the correct zigzag width to couch the cord, and pierce a hole in the tape so that the cord lies in the center of the stitching (fig 1). Use a very thin cord, such as pearl cotton or a silk yarn, and feed it from above, through the hole in the tape or the cording foot and out under the foot to the back: the cord will then be couched down in the right place automatically.

- The length of the stitch can be altered to create different effects, or you can use contrasting threads or even a monofilament nylon thread, which would be almost invisible.

- With fine fabrics, it may be necessary to use a tear-away stabilizer under the stitching to prevent puckering.

When stitching is complete, thread the ends of the cord into a large-eyed needle, and pull them through to the wrong side of the fabric.

SOUNDS GOOD, BUT WILL IT WORK?

Corded satin stitch

Satin stitch

Straight stitch

Compound whip stitch

Free-motion stitched letters

The lettering techniques below can be adapted to create any size of lettering. For all of them, the machine should be set up for free-motion stitching, with the feed teeth lowered or covered, the stitch length at 0, and no foot. The first two are worked with satin stitch and the rest with straight stitch.

Fix the fabric in an embroidery hoop for ease of maneuvering, and use a fairly thick needle: 14/90 or 16/100. Always fix the starting and finishing stitches with a few stitches on the spot.

Corded satin stitch This technique uses a very fine cord, such as pearl embroidery cotton or string.

1 Lay the cord over the lettering, and couch it in place by hand.

2 Set the zigzag width to between 3mm and 5mm (it must be wider than the cord), then loosen the needle-thread tension and tighten the bobbin tension.

3 Stitch over the cord with evenly spaced satin stitch so that the cord is completely covered.

The altered stitch tension should create a domed effect over the cord, forming a raised letter. *page 11*

Satin stitch For a slightly finer letter, use uncorded satin stitch.

1 Again, loosen the needle-thread tension, and tighten the bobbin tension.

2 Move the embroidery hoop slowly, so that the satin stitch forms evenly to create a strong line.

To form letters of an even width, the hoop may have to be turned through a full 360°. Moving the hoop sideways to work the horizontal parts of the letters will result in much finer lines, creating an italic lettering style.

Straight stitch This is the simplest stitch to use for letters, because altering the direction of stitching will not affect the final width of the letter.

1 Again, loosen the needle-thread

tension, and tighten the bobbin tension.

2 Work a few lines of straight stitch together. One line of stitching would be very fine; four or five lines are suitable for a letter ¾" (2cm) high.

Whip stitch This stitch will create a less solid letter than either of the satin-stitch methods, but because the stitching is raised it will be more defined than straight stitch.

1 This time, loosen the bobbin tension and tighten the needle-thread tension so that the top thread lies on the fabric surface and the bobbin thread is pulled up through the fabric, to create a series of little loops on the surface. (For more information on whip stitch and tension effects in general, see pages 92–93).

2 For a fine letter, work whip stitch as above, using only two rows together to form double whip stitch.

3 For a thicker letter, work a few lines of whip stitch together to create compound whip stitch.

Problem solving

• Producing attractive machine-stitched letters takes practice. In general, work a letter as you would write it. Be prepared to stop and begin a second line separately – the line which crosses an A, for example.

• Monograms that consist of two or three letters together are more attractive if the letters can be entwined in some way.

• Working lettering on a large piece of fabric, such as the tablecloth on the following pages, may involve maneuvering a large quantity of fabric at different angles. Try to roll up extra fabric and safety-pin it together to reduce the bulk.

If the quantity of your fabric is so large that you cannot maneuver it, use the satin-stitch technique described above and create italic-style letters.

pieced tablecloth

Piece together subtly contrasting shades of silk and embroider them with an eclectic selection of motifs to create a cloth fit for a feast. Select dishes from around the world, recreate a memorable meal, or concentrate on a favorite food – be it fish, as on this cloth, or an indulgent spread of delicious patisserie – or gather together the tools of the trade (see pages 106–107) and recreate them with a mixture of straight and whip stitch. Finally, label each dish or implement with a flowing script.

Stitch methods

Set straight stitch
Free-motion straight stitch
Free-motion satin stitch
Whip stitch
Vermicelli stitch
Tension: normal and altered
Feet: normal presser foot for making up
Needles: 12/80, 16/100

You will need

For a tablecloth 48" (122cm) square:
4 12" (30cm) lengths slubbed silk,
    48" (122cm) wide, in yellow, orange,
    copper, and peach
39" (100cm) gold slubbed silk,
    48" (122cm) wide
1 spool sewing thread, to piece silk
    together
Rayon machine embroidery threads in
    black, white, gold, silver, lemon,
    apricot, peach, beige, milk-chocolate
    and dark brown, light and dark gray,
    bottle-green, olive-green, and ginger
9" (23cm) embroidery hoop
5" (12cm) square cardboard template

To make the tablecloth

1 Machine wash all slubbed silks on a wool setting. Press while still damp, using a very hot, dry iron.

2 Cut out strips 5" (12cm) wide across fabric. Cut out 2 each from first 4 colors and 8 from gold. Use cardboard template to mark strips into squares, and cut out.

3 Form 12 strips of 12 squares, with a gold piece between each other color. Using set straight stitch and smaller needle, stitch squares together with a ⅜" (1cm) seam allowance. Finish seams, and press open.

4 Lay strips together to form a large square, and again stitch. Finish raw edges, and press seams open. Turn outer edges under twice to form a neat hem, and stitch all around.

To work the embroidery

1 Set machine for free-motion embroidery, and insert larger needle. Enlarge food outlines on pages 78–79 to 156%, then to 110%, using a photocopier. Transfer onto pieced fabric, using a vanishing pen and following placement plan (below). Vanishing pens fade within 48 hours, so unless you are going to work very quickly, mark position of each dish lightly in pencil, then draw fine detail with vanishing pen just before starting to embroider a dish.

2 Using alphabets on pages 104–105 or your own handwriting, draw lettering for each dish above it, again using pencil to mark its position and vanishing pen to add any detail.

3 Lettering is worked in satin stitch, food in a mixture of straight stitch, vermicelli stitch (see page 51), and whip stitch (see page 73). Use same color thread in needle and bobbin, unless a different bobbin thread would accentuate stitching. Large areas of color are worked in straight stitch with a normal needle-thread and bobbin tension, with details added on top using either straight or vermicelli stitch in a contrasting color, or whip stitch for a distinctive raised texture.

4 Insure that all ends of threads are fixed with a few stitches on the spot. When embroidery is complete, cut off all loose ends and press firmly using a very hot steam iron.

Placement plan

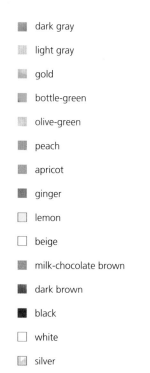

▓ dark gray

░ light gray

▓ gold

▓ bottle-green

░ olive-green

▓ peach

▓ apricot

▓ ginger

▒ lemon

☐ beige

▓ milk-chocolate brown

▓ dark brown

■ black

☐ white

▓ silver

canestrelli di chioggia
straight stitch, with whip stitch for outer shell
and gold filling

bouillabaisse de pêcheur
straight stitch, with vermicelli stitch for soup and
whip stitch on tentacles

spaghetti dela pina
straight stitch, with whip stitch for spaghetti,
shell details, and leaves

pesce alla griglia
straight stitch, with minimal whip stitch on eyes,
cut lemon, and leaves

antipasto acciughe alle olive
straight stitch for olives, with whip stitch for
detail on anchovies

moules à la marinière
straight stitch, with whip stitch on outer shells
and brown shading on *moules* detail

prawn satay
straight stitch, with whip stitch for prawn detail,
cut lemon, and leaves, and satin stitch for skewers

assiette de fruits de mer
straight stitch, with whip stitch for prawn detail,
oyster shell, and cut lemon

78

spaghetti dela pina

moules à la marinière

canestrelli di chioggia

prawn satay

pesce alla griglia

assiette de fruits de mer

antipasto acciughe alle olive

bouillabaisse

Enlarge to 156%, then to 110% on a photocopier.

vanishing fabrics

Machine embroidery is all about embellishing and adornment, adding decoration, or creating wonderful effects, and the use of vanishing fabric takes the application of embroidery techniques one step further. Instead of embroidering on a background fabric, the embroidery is worked on one of three types of vanishing fabric, and once stitching is completed, the fabric is "vanished," leaving the stitches to form a new fabric that can be as airy or as dense as the embroiderer desires.

Choosing vanishing fabric

There are three types of vanishing fabric: vanishing muslin, and hot- and cold-water soluble fabrics. Each is quite distinctive in its properties, and all have definite advantages and disadvantages, but it is worth trying all three and deciding which one best suits your style of stitching.

All three fabrics are peculiar to machine embroidery and are not widely available. Try a well-stocked notions department or needlecraft store, or look for mail-order suppliers in the advertisement section of specialized embroidery magazines.

Vanishing muslin

Vanishing muslin

Stiffened vanishing muslin was the first vanishing fabric to be developed. It can be used with or without an embroidery hoop and is a good choice for working a densely embroidered effect.

• Vanishing muslin is brittle, so if you wish to use it in a hoop, fix it correctly at the first attempt, since trying to correct it may cause tearing.
• For stitching without a hoop, use a darning foot.
• Tension settings should be normal and the fabric moved at a medium pace.
• To create a solid stitched fabric use a darning technique, with lines of stitching worked across each other.

To vanish the muslin:

1 Place the design right side down on an old towel. Press under a stationary dry iron that is set on the highest heat setting. The muslin will first turn brown, then black.

2 Remove the iron, and allow the work to cool before handling. Rub the embroidery between your hands over a wastebasket until all traces of muslin have flaked away, or brush gently with a clean, old toothbrush. Pick out any resisting bits of muslin with tweezers.

The most common mistake when vanishing the muslin is not to apply enough heat. The muslin will vanish before any natural-fiber threads and most synthetic machine-embroidery threads would be damaged. Metallic threads would be affected if next to the heat source, but if they are used on the top of the work and it is pressed on the reverse, they should be fine.

Alternatively, heat an oven to 350°F (180°C), lay the work on a baking tray and bake for five to six minutes.

Note: The dust from burnt vanishing muslin can be very irritating to asthma sufferers and may cause attacks. Also, vanishing muslin gives off an unpleasant chemical smell when heated, so work in a ventilated room.

Cold-water soluble fabric

Cold-water soluble fabric is made from seaweed. It resembles a sheet of plastic and can be rather fragile. Much less expensive than hot-water soluble fabric and more widely available, it is a good choice for open lacy effects. Cold-water soluble fabric must be used in a hoop for free-motion embroidery, since the movement of the feed teeth in set stitching would cause it to tear.

• Set stitch length at 0, and make even, medium-length stitches.
• Start by using fine machine embroidery threads, since thicker threads may cause tearing. If a small area tears, simply pin a patch over it, and proceed. If the fabric tears badly, lay the work over a double layer of the soluble fabric, and continue machine stitching.

Cold-water soluble fabric

• Straight stitch is the easiest to work, but zigzag and satin stitch are also possible. Cold-water soluble fabric is not really suitable for solid stitching, but to create small blocks, work a supporting network lines and stitch over them.

To dissolve the fabric:

1 Place the work in a bowl of cold water and agitate it gently, or hold it under a running tap. If the threads will allow, lukewarm water will dissolve the fabric more quickly.

2 Agitating in a bowl will leave a residue of soluble fabric, which can be used as a stiffener to shape the fabric. If stiffened fabric is not required, rinse thoroughly and leave to dry on an old towel.

Hot-water soluble fabric

Hot-water soluble fabric looks like a very fine silk fabric. By far the most versatile of the three vanishing fabrics for stitching purposes, it can be stretched in a hoop or used by itself for set stitching.

• Hot-water soluble fabric will take much heavier satin stitch or solid stitching than cold-water soluble fabric, but is much more expensive.

• It is strong enough to use as a base for appliqué, and since it will withstand a low ironing heat, other fabrics can be

bonded onto it using fusible web. However, the dissolving process limits the choice of appliqué fabrics and threads to those that are colorfast and can withstand boiling or simmering. In fact, most machine embroidery threads, except metallic, will withstand immersion in boiling water.

To dissolve the fabric:

1 Place the fabric in a bowl, pour a kettle of boiling water over it, and agitate. Then drain off the water. Repeat this process about five times.

Alternatively, for stubborn fabric that has no delicate stitching or appliqué, place the fabric in a saucepan of simmering water, and simmer gently for two minutes. Then drain, and repeat three times.

Another option is to lay the fabric in a large, shallow dish, cover with water, and using a low microwave setting, barely simmer the water. Remove the work as soon as the fabric starts to soften, and repeat with more water as necessary.

2 The work will look very crumpled and shrivelled when wet. It can either be dried flat and then pressed or, if necessary, it can be stretched while still wet (see page 19).

Hot-water soluble fabric

Using vanishing fabrics

The main point to remember when stitching on any of the vanishing fabrics is that the stitching lines must cross to form an interconnecting net. If they do not, when the fabric is vanished the new fabric will simply unravel into one long line of stitches. So, whatever the final design, make sure that it is supported on a grid (see left) and that the interconnecting stitch is actually across another stitch, not alongside it.

• Lines of zigzag or satin stitch must be fixed by either working them over a line of straight stitch or stitching two or more lines of straight stitch on top of them.

• Try loosening the bobbin tension slightly so that the thread appears on the upper surface; exaggerated tension settings tend to look untidy.

• Work with different-colored needle and bobbin threads. When the fabric is vanished, both will be visible.

• When working with an embroidery

hoop, you will need to fit the whole design inside the hoop, since the fabrics are likely to tear if repositioned.

Problem solving

• If the vanishing fabric is tearing or the stitches are unsatisfactory, try using a ballpoint needle or loosening top tension.

• Before cutting work out of a hoop and dissolving, hold it up to the light to check that the stitches are linked. If not, stitch a few more.

pins with panache

Work small blocks of color in jewel-bright colors, surround or divide them with grids of gold or black, and create a closely worked fabric with all the richness of a medieval tapestry. Look at stained-glass windows, Persian carpets, or Islamic mosaic work for intricate designs created with blocks of color. Embellish the embroideries with a selection of beads and transform them into exotic pins to flaunt in a hat or display as a corsage. Alternative designs can be found on page 109.

Stitch methods
Free-motion straight stitch
Free-motion satin stitch
Hand beading
Tension: normal settings throughout
Feet: darning or embroidery foot
Needle: 12/80 or 14/90

You will need
8" x 8" (20 x 20cm) vanishing muslin
5 spools machine embroidery thread, in range of colors
1 spool gold metallic machine embroidery thread
1 spool sewing thread, in outline color
Assorted beads to decorate
Hatpin and stopper, or brooch back
Beading or fine hand-sewing needle
Super-glue gel (optional)

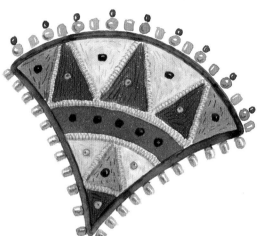

Design outlines are shown actual size.

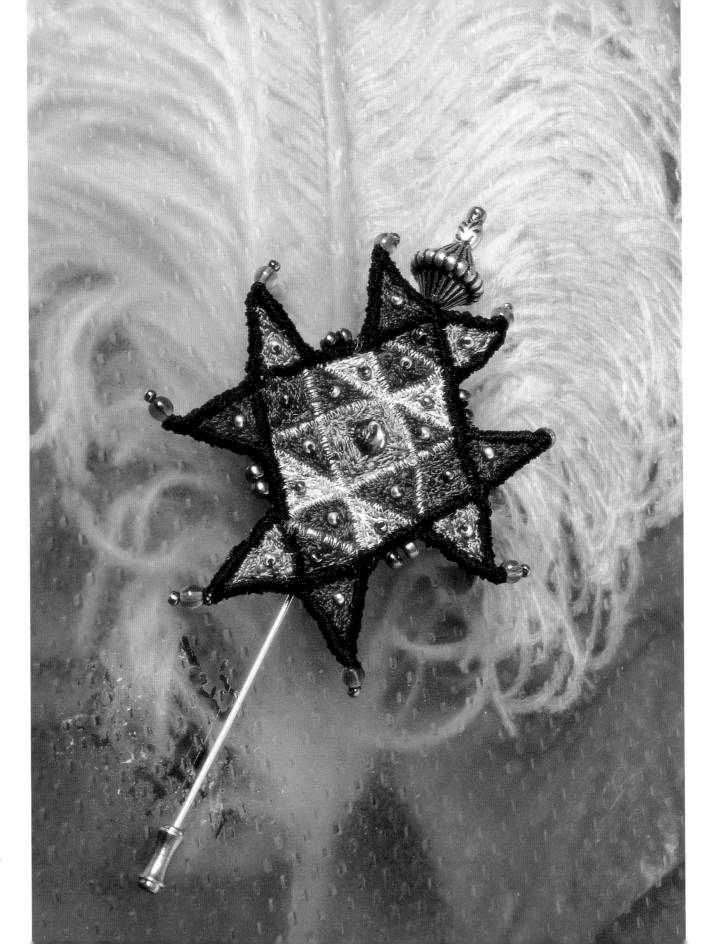

To work the embroidery

1 Draw one of the design outlines on page 82 on vanishing muslin, using a felt-tipped pen.

2 Set machine for free-motion stitching, lower or cover feed teeth, and set stitch length and zigzag to 0. Choose an embroidery thread for outline, such as charcoal used here, and use that color in bobbin throughout. Thread needle with first color of embroidery thread.

3 Start at center of each block of color and fill outline with stitches, using a darning technique. Work all blocks of one color in design, straight stitching between blocks (fig 1).

4 Change needle thread to second color and work all areas of that color. Repeat with further colors until all areas have been filled.

5 Change needle thread to gold metallic, set zigzag to 2mm, and oversew between blocks of color to divide areas (fig 2). Change needle thread to outline color, set zigzag width to 3mm, and stitch around design over outline (fig 3), finishing securely at each end.

6 Burn away vanishing muslin, using a hot iron (see page 80).

7 Thread beading or fine hand-sewing needle with a double thickness of sewing thread, make double stitches in center on back of embroidery to secure thread, then stitch on beads where shown on design outline. When beading is complete, secure end of thread with more double stitches, and snip off remaining thread.

To finish hatpin or brooch

Slide decorative beads onto hatpin, lay pin across back of embroidery, and stitch in place with a double thickness of sewing thread. If embroidery is to be used as a brooch, stick brooch back in place with super-glue gel.

fig 1

fig 2

fig 3

dancing doll

Enter into the spirit of an Edwardian theater with vanishing fabrics and glittering threads. Stitch a tiny rag doll and dress her in the finest gossamer costume, a shimmering web of embroidery topped with a bright, sparkling crown. Make her into a prima ballerina, or a slightly flushed chorus girl straight from the music halls. Allow your imagination full rein when embroidering her clothes, add wings for a magical Christmas fairy, minute stitched blossoms for a leading lady to hold, or lengthen her skirts into a sweeping train to transform her into a pouting princess.

Stitch method

Set straight stitch
Free-motion straight stitch
Free-motion satin stitch
Hand embroidery
Tension: normal settings throughout
Feet: normal presser foot
Needle: 11/80, 9/65

You will need

For a doll 7" (18cm) tall:
5" x 9½" (12 x 24cm) fine cotton fabric
   for body (a piece of old shirt dyed
   pale pink is ideal)
5½" (14cm) square pink satin for legs
Pink silk and stiffening-fabric scraps
4" (10cm) ivory fine veiling net, 36"
   (90cm) wide
10" x 20" (25 x 50cm) cold-water
   soluble fabric
Pink and ivory sewing threads
Multicolor, silver, and gold metallic
   machine embroidery threads
8" (20cm) embroidery hoop
Sewing thread for embroidering face
Assorted sewing threads for hair
Beading wire and fine steel wire
Polyester stuffing
Fine blunt screwdriver
Fine knitting needle
Hair-setting lotion
Pink nail polish
Soft pink crayon
Wooden stand (optional)
Glue

To make the doll

1 Enlarge doll outlines to 125% and clothes outlines to 156%, then to 128%, using a photocopier (see pages 88–89). Cut out doll pattern pieces. Fold pink cotton fabric right sides together, and draw upper body piece on it. With machine set for set straight stitching, size 14/90 needle, and pink sewing thread in needle and bobbin, stitch layers together just inside line, leaving waist edges open (fig 1). Fold pink satin right sides together, draw around legs piece, and repeat. Cut out body and legs pieces, clip into seam allowances at angles and curves, and turn right side out – pieces are small, so use a pin to ease turning.
2 Insert a length of beading wire from one hand across to other. Use fine steel wire to do the same for legs: if doll is to be mounted on a stand, wire in one leg should be pushed through toe to be glued into stand (fig 2).

fig 1

fig 2

3 Using screwdriver as a packing tool, stuff body and legs firmly with polyester stuffing. Stitch across legs at ankles, knees, and tops of thighs, and across arms at wrists, elbows, and tops of arms. Join body and legs at waist, fold in cut edges to create a neat join, and hand stitch together.

4 For a fuller face, cut a face piece (see below) from cotton fabric, fold cut edges under, stitch chin seam, fill with a little stuffing, and stitch to front of head with tiny hand slipstitches. Then hand embroider a simple face, and use soft pink crayon as rouge.

5 Make hair curls by twisting lengths of sewing thread around a fine knitting needle, and dampen with setting lotion. Allow to dry, remove ringlets, and hand sew hair around head.

6 Paint on shoes, using pink nail polish. When polish is dry, tie crossed threads around ankles and legs to simulate ballet slippers.

To make the doll's clothes

1 Cut out a piece of net 10" x 2½" (25 x 6cm). From remaining net, cut strips 1" (2.5cm) wide. Set stitch length to 1mm and zigzag to 2mm. With ivory thread in needle and bobbin, stitch along one long edge of a net strip, finger pleating to create a ruffle. Make 1¼yd (1m) of ruffle. Cut into 4 equal lengths.

2 Lay unstitched edge of a ruffle along lower edge of net piece, and stitch with straight stitch along zigzag line. Layer next ruffle to overlap first (fig 3), stitch, and repeat with remaining 2 ruffles to create a stiff petticoat. Fold short ends together, and hand stitch into a tube with ruffles on inside.

fig 3

face piece

upper body piece

legs piece

Enlarge doll outlines to 125% on a photocopier.

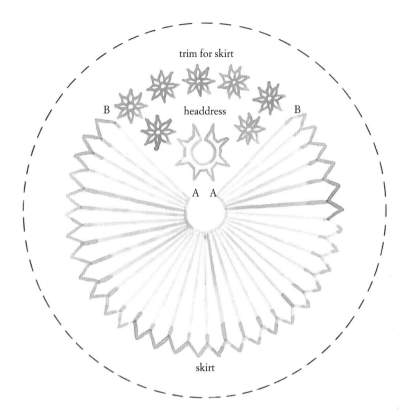

Enlarge clothes outlines to 156%, then to 128% on a photocopier.

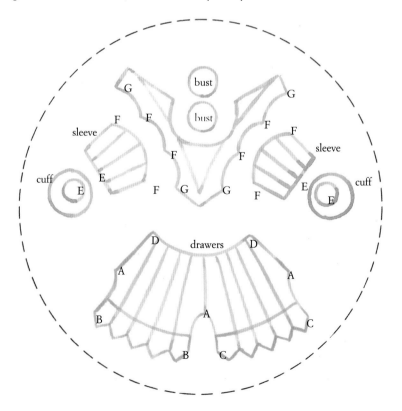

3 Remaining clothes are all stitched on soluble fabric stretched in an embroidery hoop. Lay hoop over enlarged circle pattern and trace skirt, head-dress, and trim onto soluble fabric, using a fine felt-tipped pen.

4 Remove presser foot, lower or cover feed teeth, insert 9/65 needle, and thread needle and bobbin with metallic threads: use either multicolor thread or silver thread in needle and gold on bobbin. Stitch skirt outlines first, fill in with a mesh of stitching lines and stiffen edges with zigzag set to 2mm. Stitch flower trims with gold thread in needle and bobbin, and head-dress with silver.

5 Trace remaining clothes outlines from enlarged pattern onto soluble fabric as before. For bodice, lay a piece of pink silk under hoop, right side to soluble fabric, with a piece of stiffening underneath. Using multicolored metallic thread, stitch around 3 marked triangles, and cut away excess fabric. Fill in all clothes pieces with a mesh of stitching lines as before, then stitch around neck edge of bodice with zigzag set to 2mm and using silver thread. Finally, stitch around 3 triangles to give a boned, corset effect.

6 Check that lines of stitches are interlinked (see pages 80–81), and dissolve soluble fabric. While pieces are still damp, stretch 2 bust pieces over end of a pencil to create 2 domes. When dry, stuff with pieces of bodice silk. Sew drawers and bodice into clothes (refer to outlines for guide to joining seams).

7 Dress doll, securing clothes in place with tiny hand stitches. Drawers seam is in center front; net skirt should dip down in front and flip up at back. Stitch on embroidered skirt so that net skirt is visible beneath. Put on bodice, and hand stitch bust and cuffs on. Sew on crown. Finally, stitch on skirt rosettes.

8 Fix doll to wooden stand if desired.

evening wrap

Parallel rows of straight stitching create a geometric net to hold a group of bright silk snippings. The interlocking lines of thread create a surprisingly strong fabric, which can be used as an evening shawl. Alternatively, by choosing different combinations of thread colors and fabrics, the technique could be used to make a sheer panel for a window.

Stitch methods

Set straight stitch
Set zigzag stitch
Tension: loosened bobbin tension throughout
Foot: normal presser foot
Needle: 12/80

You will need

For a shawl 78" x 17½" (200 x 44cm):
Assorted silk or fine fabrics, including narrow strips the length of finished shawl
78" x 35" (200 x 88cm) hot-water soluble fabric
2.5m (3yd) of 17½" (44cm) wide fusible web
2 large spools contrasting sewing threads

To work the net

1 Following manufacturer's instructions, back fabric pieces with fusible web. Remove paper backing, then cut out a mass of small shapes from fabric, either cutting around outlines printed on fabric or cutting out tiny scraps at random.
2 Cut out 2 pieces of soluble fabric, each 78" x 17½" (200 x 44cm). Lay fabric shapes over one piece of soluble fabric, as shown in the photograph below.
3 With iron at a low heat setting, fuse shapes to soluble fabric. Lay second piece of soluble fabric on top, and pin layers together. Using a long ruler, draw a pencil line close to one long edge.
4 Thread needle and bobbin with contrasting sewing threads. Then loosen bobbin tension slightly so that bobbin color appears on right side of fabric, set stitch length to 3mm and stitch along pencil line in as straight a line as possible.
5 Stitch lines parallel to this, approximately ¼" (6mm) apart (use presser foot as a guide), all the way across fabric. Draw a second pencil line at right angles to first across width of soluble fabric, and stitch a second set of parallel lines in the same way.
6 Using a drafsman's triangle, draw a diagonal line across one corner (fig 1), and stitch a set of parallel, diagonal lines across fabric. Draw a diagonal line in opposite direction in adjoining corner, and stitch a final set of parallel lines.
7 Remove soluble fabric as instructed on page 81. Dry, then press net.

90   fig 1

fig 2

To work the border

1 Cut out 2 border strips of fabric, each 78" (200cm) long by 3" (8cm) wide, and 2 more border strips, each 17½" (44cm) long (the stole width) by 3" (8cm) wide. Back some other strips of fabric with fusible web, and cut out 8 strips 78" (200cm) long and 8 more strips 17½" (44cm) long, both sets being ⅜" (8mm) wide. Remove backing paper.

2 Fold all border strips in half lengthwise, press, unfold, and lay first backed fabric strip alongside crease of first border strip. Lay other strips alongside, and fuse (fig 2). Set stitch length to 1mm and zigzag to 2.5mm, and sew over long cut edges with satin stitch. Repeat for remaining 3 border strips.

3 When all strips have been stitched in position, fold border strips lengthwise along pressed crease with wrong sides together. On appliquéd sides of border strips, trim raw edge outside last line of satin stitch. On other side, fold raw edge to wrong side so that back and front of border strip are the same width. Press.

4 Bind net edges with border strips. Work with right side of net and appliquéd side of strips up: net edges should be inside folded borders. Pin and baste 4 borders, then satin stitch along inner edges of border through net. Satin stitch border edges together at each corner (fig 3).

fig 3

91

tension effects

In the previous chapter we introduced the idea of using a loosened needle-thread tension to create a speckled texture and coloring in machine embroidery. The tension effects described below are created with a loosened bobbin tension and are much more exaggerated, creating exuberant stitching which can be worked to resemble hand embroidery, combined with other fabric decoration such as appliqué, or stitched in swirling lines or spirals to create glorious abstract patterns.

Using loosened bobbin tension

For anyone who has been taught sewing or has dutifully digested their sewing-machine manual, the first few stitches with a dramatically loosened bobbin tension can be quite a shock: instead of an even line of stitches, loops of the bobbin thread will be scattered across the fabric. But persevere – what may initially look like a mistake can be refined into a variety of distinct and delightful stitch effects.

Practice the different stitches below to discover the extent of your machine's capabilities: there will come a point when the tension difference will be too great and one thread will continually snap. Then use the different effects selectively to add a joyful abandon to more sedate projects.

Setting up the machine

Set the machine for free-motion stitching, with feed teeth lowered or covered, stitch length set at 0, and no foot, but remember to lower the presser bar. Use a slightly thicker needle than normal: 14/90 or 16/100.

Start with the zigzag width set at 0, but then experiment with different widths. For first experiments, fit the fabric in an embroidery hoop, and use different colors of needle and bobbin thread so that it is quite obvious which thread is which.

Tension

Individual adjustments will be described for each effect, but it is important to remember two points:
• There must be some tension for the machine to work properly: if both needle-thread and bobbin tensions are completely loose, the threads will disappear into the shuttle race and break.

• Although the two tensions are adjusted separately, altering one always affects the other. If one is loosened, the effect will be enhanced by tightening the other, and if one is tightened and the other is not loosened, the tightened thread will try to pull the other through the fabric, but because there is no give the thread being pulled is likely to break.

Starting to stitch

Whip stitch

If the bobbin tension is loosened and the needle-thread tension tightened, the needle thread will lie on the fabric surface and the bobbin thread will whip around it.

Practice stitching at different speeds and moving the hoop more and less quickly to create different lengths of stitch. Stitching on the spot with a loosened bobbin tension can create decorative knots but is wearing on the needle thread, which may break.

Feather stitch

Feather stitch is an exaggerated version of whip stitch, achieved with a very loose bobbin tension and tight needle-thread tension. Stitch quickly to create the distinctive loops on the fabric surface.

This stitch is best worked in whirls or circles, because straight lines tend to unravel. If straight lines are desired, after stitching paint the wrong side with a rubber-based craft glue. Alternatively, iron a strip of fusible interfacing over the back of the stitches.

Whip stitch

Feather stitch

Cording

Cable stitch

Loose zigzag

Loose tailor tacking

Cording

With the tensions set for whip stitch, practice working tiny stitches so that the bobbin thread completely wraps the needle thread, creating a corded effect. It may help to loosen the bobbin tension or to tighten the needle-thread tension; the effect can be increased by using a heavier needle thread, which will automatically tighten the top tension.

Cable stitch

Cable stitch can resemble cording, but is worked in reverse: the bobbin is wound with thick thread, and the tension settings are altered to create a loosened needle-thread tension and slightly tightened bobbin tension, so that the bobbin thread remains below the surface and the needle thread is pulled down to wrap around it. The fabric is stitched wrong side up so that when it is turned over the thicker bobbin thread lies on the the right side.

Quite thick threads, including cotton knitting yarns and embroidery threads, can be wound around the bobbin by hand. Avoid any fluffy or knobby threads, but otherwise, if it will pull through the delivery eye on the case, it should stitch.

Experiment: using a heavy bobbin thread may be enough on its own to pull the top thread down. Once a satisfactory effect has been perfected, try using looser needle-thread tensions to create a feather stitch, or loosen the bobbin tension further to allow the bobbin thread to twist on the lower surface.

Loose zigzag

Working zigzag stitch with a loose bobbin tension and tight needle-thread tension can create a variety of effects.

If the bobbin tension is loosened slightly and the needle-thread tension tightened slightly, the effect will be a bicolored, fairly flat stitch. If the bobbin tension is quite loose and the needle-thread tension tight, the distinct zigzag will disappear, and instead the bobbin thread will form uneven horizontal straight stitches and the top thread a slightly meandering line in the center.

Loose tailor tacking

Using a tailor-tacking foot (which automatically creates a line of loops) with a loosened bobbin tension and tightened needle-thread tension will create an extravagant mass of loops. The stitches are so loose that it is quite easy to pull out the top thread gently and leave two distinct rows of loops.

Whether the top thread is in or out, the stitches are quite vulnerable. Either fix them on the wrong side by painting with a rubber-based glue or ironing on a strip of iron-on interfacing, or trap them under a bonded layer of organza (see pages 94–96).

Problem solving

• Breaking threads are the most common problem, and are usually caused by one tension being tightened without the other being loosened.
• Using different weights of thread may cause problems – try a larger needle for the top thread. Heavy bobbin threads in a loosened bobbin case may cause the screw to work its way out. If so, replace it immediately.
• When using unusual threads, listen carefully to the machine. If it sounds labored or makes a clunk, stop, and investigate. Most problems are likely to be caused by fluff in the bobbin shuttle or a loose thread catching, but trying to force the stitching will pull the shuttle race out of alignment.

table settings

One of the great advantages of machine embroidery is that although some of the effects can look quite ethereal, the machine stitching means that it is actually very strong, so if you choose washable fabrics and use mercerized threads the finished items will be relatively hardwearing despite their delicate appearance. This final project uses a combination of tension techniques and shadow effects to create table settings for the seriously stylish. The embroidered effects were worked without an embroidery hoop, but for less experienced stitchers a hoop might be a help.

Stitch methods
Set straight stitch
Free-motion straight stitch
Free-motion satin stitch
Tension: normal and loosened bobbin tension
Feet: tailor-tacking foot; normal presser foot for making up
Needle: 12/90

You will need
For 4 napkins and rings:
4 different-colored pieces lightweight cotton fabric, each 6" x 10" (15 x 25cm)
4 pieces contrast-colored organzas, each 6" x 10" (15 x 25cm)
20" x 12" (50 x 30cm) fusible web
Silk, velvet, and satin scraps
1¼ yd (1m) square plain fabric, for napkins
8" x 7" (20 x 18cm) lining fabric, for rings
Sewing threads in assorted colors, including napkin color
Thicker bobbin thread
Monofilament nylon thread
Rubber-based craft glue
For 1 table mat:
20" x 14" (50 x 35cm) each colored cotton fabric, contrasting organza, fusible web, lining fabric
Silk, velvet, and satin scraps
Assorted sewing threads
Thicker bobbin thread
20" x 14" (50 x 35cm) paper

Layering and embroidering the fabric
The fabric for the outside of napkin rings, the appliqué on napkins, and the mat is formed in the same way and then made up into individual items. Contrasting scraps are trapped between the base cotton fabric and organza, and embroidery can be worked both on base cotton and over the organza, creating a multicolored layered fabric.

1 Stitch some random lines of embroidery on colored cotton fabric, using a selection of the tension effects described on pages 92–93.

2 Lay embroidered fabric on a flat surface for ironing: use an ironing board for small pieces, and place several layers of towels or blankets on a table for larger ones.

3 Cut out tiny scraps of fabric to trap. Scraps can be laid on cotton and under fusible web, and will be seen under layer

of organza, or can be laid on fusible web and will initially be under organza, but organza can then be carefully cut away to reveal true color of fabric scrap. Lay down some scraps, reserving any scraps in velvet or with raised effects for revealing later.

4 Remove paper backing from fusible web, and lay it over the cotton. Lay more scraps of fabric on web, lay down random lengths of colored cotton thread if desired, lay organza on top, and fuse by ironing again. Melting of adhesive web will bond fabrics tightly together and may cause a slight marbling or graduation of color.

5 Using sharp embroidery scissors, cut away organza above second layer of scraps (on top of fusible web). Cut edges can be left, or they can be outlined with a loosened zigzag.

6 Stitch more random lines of embroidery over organza, using tension effects described on pages 92–93.

To make the napkin ring

1 Cut out a strip of layered fabric 7¼" x 2¼" (18.5 x 5.5cm). Fold ¼" (5mm) to wrong side on 1 short and 2 long edges, and press.

2 Cut out a strip of lining 7" x 2" (18 x 5cm) and a strip of fusible web 6½" x 1½" (17 x 4cm). Lay fusible web in center of wrong side of lining, iron to fuse, and remove backing paper. Fold ¼" (5mm) overlap of lining over web along all edges.

3 With fusible web down, lay lining strip on wrong side of layered strip, with short folded-over ends even and lining central on layered strip along length (fig 1).

Iron to fuse. Thread machine with monofilament thread in needle and bobbin, adjust for set stitching, and stitch along lining edge from uneven end to ¼in (5mm) from even ends, across strip, back along other edge, and finally across to start of stitching.

4 Following manufacturer's instructions, apply craft glue carefully and sparingly to both sides of unfolded end of layered fabric, and insert between lining and layered fabric to form a ring (fig 2). Hold together tightly until glued.

To make the napkins

1 Cut out napkin fabric into 4 even squares. Fold over a narrow double hem around each square, thread machine with thread to match napkin fabric in needle and bobbin, and stitch with straight stitch.

2 From remnants of layered fabric used for napkin rings, cut out 4 2½" (6.5cm) squares. On each, cut a gentle curve from opposite corners to make a quarter circle shape.

3 Appliqué a quarter circle at the corner of each napkin, using set zigzag stitch.

To make the mat

1 Fold paper rectangle into quarters, and cut away a gentle curve at free corners to make a pleasing oval.

2 Use this pattern to cut out a layered oval and a lining oval.

3 With right sides together, lay ovals one on the other, and sew all around with a ⅝" (1.5cm) seam allowance, leaving a gap for turning. Trim and notch seam allowance all around, turn right side out. Press. Slipstitch gap closed by hand.

fig 1

fig 2

Motifs & stitch samplers

On the following pages you will find a selection of alternative designs or motifs for some of the projects in the book. These include a selection of quilting patterns; two stitching samplers that provide suitable outlines for practicing free-motion stitching techniques; two alphabets, one with upright letters, both large and small, ideal for initials or bold lettering and a second more flowing one with letters suitable for monograms, names, or messages; a superb spread of motifs for the Pieced Tablecloth; and alternative designs for the Button Collection, and Pins with Panache.

quilting motifs

See Summer, Winter Bedspread on page 40

The top quilt on pages 40–41 is quilted by stitching around the printed flowers on the fabric, but not all fabrics are printed with such suitable patterns. If you would rather quilt a plain fabric, a tiny check, or an allover pattern, choose one of the patterns shown here. Enlarge to the desired size using a photocopier, and transfer the full-size pattern onto thin cardboard to use as a template. Draw around the template on the fabric using a vanishing pen or a sharp, hard pencil to create a pattern around which to quilt. If you are not sure how many patterns to draw, use the template to cut out a number of paper shapes and lay them on the quilt to create a pleasing design.

straight-stitch sampler

The outlines given here are intended for practicing the free-motion machine embroidery techniques with a darning foot described on pages 44–45 and the free-motion embroidery techniques with no foot on pages 50–51. The four corner designs are intended as stitching suggestions only, and there is no need to transfer them onto fabric – just try to reproduce them with stitching. The geometric or pictorial patterns could be transferred (see pages 18–19) and then filled with stitches. Either work the motifs on scraps of fabric, or work them all on a piece of calico to form a sampler.

satin-stitch sampler

The stitching suggestions and outlines here are intended for practicing free-motion stitching techniques using zigzag and satin-stitch settings, as described on page 60. The four corner designs are stitching suggestions to practice and perhaps use as filling techniques for larger areas. When working satin-stitch daisies or beads of color, remember that the needle only swings from side to side, so to create petals radiating all around a center or beads lying at different angles, the fabric must be moved.

alphabets

See Pieced Tablecloth on page 74

The lettering used on the Pieced Tablecloth on pages 74–79 is the designer's own handwriting, written large. If you wish to embroider the words on the tablecloth, romantic messages on a pillowcase, names on laundry bags or other words, either write them yourself or use the flowing script provided here (below). To use the lower script for the tablecloth, enlarge it to the desired size on a photocopier. The top alphabet with the fine letters would be easy to work in couching (see page 72) or either of the straight-stitch methods described on page 73. The lower, more flowing, italic-like script would be better worked with one of the satin-stitch methods on page 73.

F G H I J K L
Q Q R S T U V
a b c d e f g h i j k l
u v v w x y z ⁓

I J K L L M N O P Q
a b c d e f g h i j k l m n o
3 4 4 5 6 6 7 8 8 9 0

tools of the trade

See Pieced Tablecloth on page 74

The Pieced Tablecloth on pages 74–79 is covered with wonderful fishy dishes, but it could just as well be embroidered with a selection of other designs. A striking alternative to food, but with similar gastronomic appeal, would be a selection of kitchen implements. You could use some of these motifs to embroider a tea cozy, the backs of oven gloves, a shelf edging, or pillows. Enlarge the motifs if necessary, using a photocopier.

button &
brooch
alternatives

See Button Collection on page 62 and
Pins with Panache on page 82

The stars, flowers, or simple stripes shown
here would all be suitable designs to use
as alternatives to the heart designs on
the buttons in the collection on pages
62–63; to use on 1⅛" (29mm) buttons,
reduce to 64% on a photocopier. Or use
any of the round designs for brooches
worked on vanishing muslin, following
the instructions for Pins with Panache on
pages 82–85. There are also two
alternative pin designs. The dots around
the designs on the right indicate the
position for beads and are not intended
to be stitched!